THE
SEEKING

THE
SEEKING

Discovering spiritual truths over
three days with Ramesh Balsekar

YogiImpressions®

YogiImpressions®

THE SEEKING

First published in India in 2004 by
Yogi Impressions Books Pvt. Ltd.
1711, Centre 1, World Trade Centre,
Cuffe Parade, Mumbai 400 005, India.
Website: www.yogiimpressions.com

First Edition, March 2004
Fifth reprint, July 2014

Cover and Interior Book Design: Shiv Sharma

ISBN 978-81-88479-58-0

Is there any such thing as free will?

Is everything in life predetermined?

Does God play dice with the universe?

CONTENTS

FOREWORD

The idea of an unedited presentation of Ramesh Balsekar's daily talks came to me during my visit to Ramesh in 2003. While reading a book, you can move at your own pace and need not miss a single word.

The question arose... how many days to record? Ramesh said: "3 days is enough." But which 3 days? Any 3 days? Why not take the first 3 days of my visit? Done!

Here it is then. A taste of Ramesh's talks that happened to cover his main concepts. I thankfully acknowledge the dedicated efforts of Kali Orneales in making this book happen.

That a taxi driver outside my hotel in Mumbai, after my probably confusing directions of where to go, answered "Oh, you go to Ramesh Baba!" really made the third day.

Those of you who want more of Ramesh will find it – only if it is God's Will.

Göran Ekdahl
Mumbai, July 2003

Day 1

Ramesh: Your name is?

Rajhans: Rajhans.

Ramesh: What part of the world are you from?

Rajhans: Australia.

Ramesh: Australia. I see. What do you do in Australia?

Rajhans: I am a lawyer.

Ramesh: Lawyer. I see. So I should be careful.

Rajhans: Not yet. (Laughter)

Ramesh: Yes, Rajhans?

Rajhans: The two areas that seem to come up very strongly in my life...

Ramesh: Is this the first day you are here? Have you heard me before?

Rajhans: I came once – yesterday. That is the first time I have ever seen you.

Ramesh: So, you heard what I had to say. Any reaction?

Rajhans: Yes, these two areas, these are the reactions. Although I can intellectually understand what you are saying and have heard it in different ways before, part of the difficulty that I have is in actually accepting or believing. The area around 'doing' and 'us not being the doers' is an area that I can understand, but actually in terms of believing it or feeling it as a way of life, that I find difficult to understand.

Ramesh: I see... I see. Now, earlier what you understood, you have heard it before. Have you heard before that 'you find out exactly what you are looking for?' What does enlightenment mean for you? The spiritual seeking is seeking enlightenment. What does the seeker expect enlightenment to do for him, for the rest of his life? Have you heard that before?

Rajhans: Well, yes. First I had rather immature views of what that might be... Nirvana, life without any problems, etc.

Ramesh: That is not true. That is not correct. Nirvana is not going to make the rest of your life free of any problems. Impossible.

Rajhans: But as I have gotten more older, it has been one way I have recognized that enlightenment is something that is achieved by actual work and witnessing or viewing exactly what you are doing in your life. Then I find that I spend time like I do with you or with other people. Even during holidays, when I am in complete relaxation, where I feel that the identification with 'doing', with other people's issues and with emotional things is not there.

Ramesh: Now when you are on a holiday you say you are relaxed, then you say, the identification is not there? That means Rajhans is no longer there as a separate entity? What is identification?

Rajhans: It means that I am... I feel like I am flowing with the moment. I don't feel like I am mind-f**king.

Ramesh: Yes, but who? Somebody is flowing. Rajhans is flowing. Who is flowing? So, Rajhans knows that at a certain time he has the feeling of flowing. Rajhans feels that 'he' has the feeling of flowing. So Rajhans is still there, very much identified with a particular name and form, as a separate entity.

Rajhans: At the time that is happening, I am not aware that it is Rajhans or anybody else. I am just there.

Ramesh: So, 'who' is the one who is there? 'Me'! The 'me' is Rajhans.

Rajhans: I am not even aware that it is 'me' at the time. At the time, I am just moving through and moving through my life.

Ramesh: Yes.

Rajhans: All right? It is at the times I find that I am not relaxed, or when I am identified, that actually I am starting to see that there is almost a person separate from me.

Ramesh: In other words, what you are saying Rajhans is, you realize that Rajhans is uncomfortable. When Rajhans is comfortable, Rajhans is not particularly aware of his being comfortable.

Rajhans: That is right.

Ramesh: But it is Rajhans who is sometimes comfortable, sometimes uncomfortable. So, my point, Rajhans, is a very basic point, that is why I am laboring it, and that is: identification with a particular name and form as a separate entity is the very basis of life. So, whether it is Jesus Christ or the Prophet or whoever we regard as a Sage, as a self-realized being, so long as that person is alive, identification with a particular name and form as a separate entity has to be there. Ramana Maharshi, whoever you regard as a Sage, any Sage, during his lifetime responded to his name being called. The fact that a Sage responds to his name being called means, obviously, that there is identification with a particular body and a name as a separate individual entity, you see?

So, therefore, my basic point is that identification as a separate entity cannot be lost, whether you are a Sage or not, until the body is dead. The identification with a particular body and name and form is the ego. The point I am laboring at the moment is, no one can lose his ego! No one can lose his identification as a separate entity unless the body is dead. You see? So, losing one's identity as a criterion for self-realization I simply cannot accept, otherwise the Sage would have gone about like a zombie! 'No identification as a separate entity', so somebody would say: 'Hey you!' and touch, then he would turn because he was touched. So what I am saying, I repeat, even a Sage at any time during his lifetime responds to his name being called. Therefore, there is identification with a particular name and form as a separate entity. Therefore, the identification can never ever be lost so long as the body is alive.

Identification with a particular body as a separate individual is the ego. So my basic point, Rajhans, is, if a Sage responds to his name being called and, therefore, there is a separate entity and the ordinary person responds to his name being called and both suffer the same kind of pains in the moment, or enjoy pleasure in the moment, where is the difference? Egos exist in both cases. They respond in both cases. Both enjoy the pleasure of the moment and suffer the pain of the moment, therefore, where is the difference between the two egos? That is my basic question! Do you see what I mean?

Rajhans: Yes, I do.

Ramesh: And that, according to my concept, is: the 'sense of personal doership'. Both are egos, but the Sage's ego has been able totally to accept 'no one is a doer' whereas the ordinary person's ego, the ordinary ego, has not been able to accept totally that 'there is no doer!' That is the difference. Therefore, the basis of enlightenment or self-realization, the difference between the two egos, is represented in my concept by the 'sense of personal doership'. In other words what I am saying is: remove the sense of personal doership in an ordinary ego and he has become a Sage! Remove the sense of personal doership totally from any ego and he becomes a Sage. Is that concept of enlightenment or self-realization acceptable to you, Rajhans? Now, you say you have been to many people, read many books?

Rajhans: I have read many books.

Ramesh: When did this seeking begin, Rajhans? Many years ago?

Rajhans: It started around 1989, 1990.

Ramesh: Oh, I see. Not too long ago. Thirteen years I mean, it depends, thirteen years can seem like thirty years. Now, where has that course of seeking taken you? Whose books have you read? What teachings have you gone through?

Rajhans: I have mainly read Osho and also Ramana Maharshi and also your own and other books which...

Ramesh: Have you read Krishnamurti?

Rajhans: No, I haven't.

Ramesh: Gurdjieff?

Rajhans: Yes, some of it.

Ramesh: So having read all that, my question is, Rajhans, what do you think the spiritual seeker is seeking enlightenment for? What does the average seeker, spiritual seeker, expect enlightenment, self-realization, truth, ultimate understanding, whatever you call it, what does the average seeker expect self-realization to do for him for the rest of his life?

Rajhans: For me, it is clarity.

Ramesh: I see. Clarity of what? Clarity of the understanding?

Rajhans: Clarity of the understanding, and devotion, and also clarity of 'a oneness' with what is happening.

Ramesh: So, clarity of 'a oneness' with the Source. Oneness with God. Now, 'clarity of oneness with God', how will that help you, Rajhans, to live the rest of your life... in what way better than it was before? That is my core question about seeking. Do you see what I mean?

Rajhans: I suppose for me, to answer your question, for me that feels like an absence for me. That is the only way I can explain.

Ramesh: Quite right. That is, I am afraid, that is the concept. That is the understanding. Rajhans disappears. My point then is: if Rajhans disappears, who continues his practice as a lawyer? If Rajhans has disappeared... Do you have a family?

Rajhans: I have an extended family, but I am not married.

Ramesh: So, who lives his life with his extended family? Who carries on his practice as a lawyer? There is no Rajhans! If there is no Rajhans, who lives his life? Who does his practice? Whatever it is, you are a lawyer, someone is a doctor, someone is a banker, someone is a tailor. So, the occupation whatever it is, if Rajhans disappears, then who lives the rest of his life?

So my basic concept is, even if there is enlightenment or self-realization, it is an impersonal happening. It is a happening. So somebody has a heart operation, somebody's appendix has been removed, somebody has another kind of operation but he continues to live his life exactly as before. Doing whatever he was doing before. And my point is, the heart operation has happened, enlightenment has happened! One is physical, the other we can say is mental. But the one who has had the heart operation has to live his life for the rest of that life. So a person who has had this spiritual operation still has to live his life. You see? So the spiritual operation that has happened, how does it help the spiritual patient to live the rest of his life in any sense better, smoother? In what way is the spiritual seeker, when he is successful in his quest, helped to live the rest of his life?

My whole point, Rajhans, is: this is basic and it has been totally ignored. Why? For the simple reason you have just mentioned, that once enlightenment has happened Rajhans will no longer be concerned with his life. Not true. And because of this illusory aim of self-realization, a lot of confusion and frustration exists amongst seekers, according to my concept, for this precise reason. People come here and they say: 'I have come here because I am frustrated. I have been a spiritual seeker for thirty years. I have done this, I have done that and nothing has happened.' And the words are actually: 'Nothing has changed!' Do you see what I mean, Rajhans? 'Nothing has changed.' Therefore, I ask: 'What did you expect to change?'

What did you expect enlightenment to do for you? What do *you* expect enlightenment to do for *you*?

Rajhans: I suppose that part for me is not getting sucked into the emotions that I have going on, and how to deal with those emotions when they occur and not get sucked in.

Ramesh: So... I keep pressing on this point. Rajhans who came here says, 'Yes that is true. I am looking for something. I am looking for something!' And what am I looking for? What I have put into words. What every spiritual seeker is truly looking for, whether he knows it or not, is to be anchored in peace. You can use some other word, to be anchored in peace while facing life from moment to moment. With the total acceptance no one can change what the next moment is going to bring for anybody. The next moment may bring for me pleasure or pain. So, what I expect self-realization to do for me is to enable me to live my life, accepting whatever the moment brings, because I have no choice and yet feel anchored in peace and harmony. Do you see?

So, then what does being anchored in peace and harmony – lovely phrase, very attractive – what does it really mean in practical life? In daily living what does it mean? What it means, according to my concept, is you live your life accepting whatever the moment brings but you leave whatever happens in the moment with the moment. If there is pleasure you enjoy the pleasure and forget it. If there is pain you suffer the pain and forget it. You do not carry on in horizontal time, and you carry it on in horizontal time only if you say, 'I had this pleasure this moment, what can I do to make it last? I have suffered pain in the moment, what can I do to ensure that it doesn't happen again?' Do you see? Either way this sense of 'What can I do to prolong it or to stop it' is the basis of why you cannot leave whatever is in the moment to the moment. That means a great deal of pressure. Mental stress. This doership.

My point is, how do you know what you are looking for is real? Real in phenomenal life. How do you know it is not an illusion? That is the second point. And the answer to that is, 'I know it is not an illusion because I have experienced it. When I am on a holiday, when I am resting, I have had the feeling of floating with life. I have had the sensation that this moment, what I have, is what I want for the rest of my life.' You see? You have had the experience, therefore, you can know that it is available in this life. When you had that why did you lose it? You see? This is truly spiritual seeking and, in spiritual seeking, you have to do the seeking yourself I am afraid. Whatever others tell you is their concept.

So the question that I come down to is, when I had that experience and I know what I want, why did I lose it? Why did you lose it? Think of it, Rajhans, and you will come to the conclusion, every time you had that feeling some thought has shattered it. You had that experience; a thought comes 'Oh! I left something undone in the office', that feeling you have may be stirred, but it is not shaken, it is not broken. Similarly other thoughts happen, which are on the surface, they may stir your feeling but they don't shake you out of it. That feeling is not shattered. Therefore, what kind of thought has in your own experience shattered the peace you were enjoying in the moment? And you will find, if you go into it, that the thought which has shattered your peace in the moment is a thought of something you did in the past – the past may be twenty years ago, ten years ago or last week – something you did last week, or ten years ago, which you know you should not have done or something you could have done for your friend and did not do.

To take an extreme case, you remember the time a friend came to you for help, he wanted to borrow a large sum of money which could have changed his life forever, big business opportunity, big investment opportunity, he knew and you knew that you could have lent him the money but you didn't. Whatever reason, mainly because you were afraid the money may not be returned to you and you can't afford to lose a large amount. Whatever the reason, you did not give him the money and the poor beggar was so sensitive, over-sensitive, that when he lost his big chance he committed suicide. I am taking an extreme case. Therefore, that thought of someone you could have helped and didn't help and which led to his death brings about a feeling of guilt and shame. Or another thought comes, the other way around. Somebody could have helped you and didn't, so that you lost the biggest opportunity in your life. Since then you have always hated the man. In fact, you hate him so much every time the name is mentioned, whether it belongs to him or not, it makes you hate the man.

Therefore, my point is, what surely breaks the foundation of that peace in the moment is a thought of something you did and you should not have done, or something you could have done and did not do – shame and guilt. Or a thought of hatred and malice towards someone, exactly the same thing, who did to you what he should not have done, or did not do for you what he could have done. So you go into it, make your own research and I can tell you, with confidence, that the thought which truly shatters the peace everyone has enjoyed sometime or the other, is a thought of shame and guilt for one's action, or lack of action, or hatred and malice towards the other for the same reason.

In other words, the Buddha said, he gave straight away the question, 'What will enlightenment do for me?' He said, 'Enlightenment means the end of suffering.' Straight. Enlightenment means the end of suffering. So we have to find out what Buddha means by suffering. Buddha was no fool. He knew from personal experience that even after his total Understanding, he could never know what the next moment will bring and if the next moment is suffering, pain, it has to be accepted and the pain has to be suffered. Knowing that, Buddha categorically and boldly says, 'Enlightenment is the end of suffering' and my interpretation of what Buddha meant is, 'Enlightenment, total self-realization that no one is a doer, neither me nor the other, removes the suffering which smashes the foundation of the peace whenever I have it.' And that suffering is the enormous, massive load everyone carries. A load of shame and guilt for one's own action, and hatred and malice for the other's action.

Remove this load and you truly do not have to wait for the peace to occur. Remove this burden of pride and arrogance for good deeds, shame and guilt for the bad ones, hatred and malice towards the other. Remove that burden and you will find that you do not have to look for peace; absence of this load *is* the presence of what I am looking for. See what I mean? That is my concept, Rajhans.

You will have to examine this concept for yourself out of your own experience, and then decide whether this concept of mine is acceptable to you or not. And if you accept my concept for what it is worth at the moment, when you leave here you will question the concept and not be able to accept it. Therefore, what I am saying is, I do not want you, for your own sake, to be misguided by my concept. I do not want you to be brainwashed, therefore, I am telling you, this is a concept I offer to you in all faith.

It is for you to investigate that concept from your own experience and find out whether it is possible at all to accept 'No one is a doer'. It is possible, because we know several people who have been able to do that and we have been able to recognize the fact that while they suffer the same kinds of pains as I do and enjoy the same pleasures as I do, it is clear that they seem to be anchored in peace and harmony, they deal with the moment as the moment. Therefore, you know that it can be done. You know that it is possible to live without the sense of personal doership. It is not only possible to live without the sense of personal doership but also to live your life with a great deal of smoothness, ease, no physical strain and no mental stress. My concept, Rajhans, is this is precisely what the spiritual seeker is seeking without realizing exactly what he is seeking.

Therefore, I put it to you, according to my concept, all that any spiritual seeker can have is just this – never being uncomfortable with myself, never having to hate myself for anything, never having to be uncomfortable with the other, never having to hate the other. That is all! If out of self-realization you expect much more than that then you will have to look elsewhere, my concept will not help you.

So now, with this, what was your question, Rajhans?

Rajhans: This moment, I answer, I feel quite connected as I speak to you.

Ramesh: Do you feel quite connected with the concept?

Rajhans: Yes, yes.

Ramesh: I see, but what you said is a valid problem: you were able to accept it intellectually. 'If I can accept this concept intellectually and it removes my whole burden of shame and guilt and hatred, I would like that. Therefore, intellectually I cannot not accept the concept.' Intellectually, no reasonable person could reject that concept but, in order to be effective, the understanding has to be total. Total acceptance of 'No one is a doer', without any question. Someone asked me, 'Is there a test for it? Is there a test for me to find out if my acceptance is total?' and I said, 'Yes, I was told there is something called a truth serum which I am injected with and, after it had its effect, someone asks me a question and I cannot but give a true answer.' So if you want to test yourself go through that. Go to a doctor and if he says, 'I can give you this truth serum quite safely with one hundred percent safety, it will last for twenty minutes and in the twenty minutes you cannot speak a lie.' Then have the doctor give you that and have the doctor ask you, 'Have you truly been able to accept no one is a doer absolutely?', and the truth will come out.

Rajhans: (Laughing)

ﷺ

Ramesh: Yes, I forget your name.

Ashwin: Ashwin.

Ramesh: From Singapore? Yes, Ashwin?

Ashwin: *This truth serum thing...*

Ramesh: May not be a hundred percent...

Ashwin: *(Laughing) No, no. Not that.*

Ramesh: *(Laughs)* That is why I am told that it is not accepted in the courts.

Ashwin: *My question is, even if there is an answer, a truthful answer, isn't it the intellectual understanding which is giving the outcome? The answer is basically from the intellectual understanding.*

Ramesh: No. The answer then would be, 'I am intellectually able to accept it, deep down I don't know!', that would be the answer. The answer would not be 'Of course I have to accept, I do accept no one is a doer'; otherwise the truth would be 'Intellectually I accept it. I would love to have it throughout but I am still, at the moment, not able to tell you that I truly believe in it.' That would be the answer.

Ashwin: *Can I question you on this?*

Ramesh: Please, please.

Ashwin: *In spite of what you say... I mean we say that most of us have these peaceful experiences, and they are disturbed by some thought, and the reason why these peaceful instances are disturbed are basically because of some thoughts coming from personal doership. Now you said that leave this personal doership and you will have more of peace.*

Ramesh: Yes.

Ashwin: *In literature, I mean in spiritual literature there is, however, a lot of importance, or importance in terms of the pinnacle of achievement, given to a moment or a transition which causes this change. Why is that?*

Ramesh: That is because what is the basis of non-doership? The basis of non-doership is, whatever happens in life... the basis of non-doership is what the Buddha said, 'Events happen, deeds are done but there is no individual doer thereof.' So, if there is no individual doer thereof, whatever happens at any moment through whichever body-mind organism is a happening which had to happen, which could not *not* happen according to a Cosmic Law. Call it God's Will or according to a Cosmic Law. So, everything that happens has to happen but it is not anybody's doing. So, everything *has* to happen is the basis.

Nothing can happen unless it is God's Will or Cosmic Law. A law according to which everything in the universe has been moving precisely the way it is supposed to move.

Ashwin: The other way I would put a question is, you know... one in a million is going to be enlightened, so for an individual that accepts the one in a million probability...

Ramesh: All right. Forget the one in a million. Even if it happens with one in a million, fine! But what I am saying is, even the intellectual acceptance of it can give you a lot of relief from mental stress. How does it work? I will tell you how it works. If there is a total acceptance no question about it, but if it is only intellectual acceptance in the course or process of its being deeper, during that process what happens is, for example, on a conceptual scale of zero to ten, you have that peace, a thought occurs and as soon as a thought occurs before your peace is truly shattered, you are struggling with that and that involvement goes on zero, one, two, three, four and even the intellectual acceptance is more than likely to cut off the involvement maybe at eight, nine or even ten and, then as the intellectual understanding goes deeper, more and more by personal experience, the involvement getting cut off happens quicker and quicker, earlier and earlier.

When you find the involvement getting cut off at three, four, three, four, something like that, then you begin to say, 'Who cares if it is not zero?' You are quite satisfied with the involvement getting cut off at two, three, four and when your acceptance is, 'Who cares what it is' then it will happen because your expectation, which is the biggest handicap, is no longer there. 'I want total enlightenment', when that demand for it is not there, when you say 'Who cares? If it is to happen, let it happen' then from three or four there can be a quantum jump to zero.

Ashwin: Can I express my gratitude and, at the same time, ask what have you done to me?

Ramesh: (*Laughing*) What I have done to you only you will know. Better or worse, let me confess.

Ashwin: Because if I go according to my old ways, I mean most of the questions when they arise, the answers are there somewhere.

Ramesh: That is right. The answers arise. Maybe at one, two, three, maybe later, but the answers arise.

Ashwin: And the worst part is, as per the old habits, whenever you go to a place of worship, you stand in front of the deity either asking for grace, asking for this, asking for that and I can't do that because...

Ramesh: What is wrong with it? What is wrong with you not being able to beg for favors from God?

Ashwin: Yes, that is what I am saying... there is nothing wrong.

Ramesh: Then?

Ashwin: It is just that...

Ramesh: It happens, you see? Fine. It is more than likely to happen. What does it mean? Your not being ready to beg favors from God, it simply means you have surrendered your free will to God, 'God do what you like with this object which you have created!'

Ashwin: Yes, but it is not complete. There is always this desire about to come out and it sort of...

Ramesh: Wanting to beg is an involvement but it cuts off, quite right! That is what I am saying. The involvement just cuts off.

Ashwin: I don't know where in the scale of ten, but it is quite confusing because you are neither there, neither...

Ramesh: Therefore, my point is, accept the confusion. Accept the confusion! Accept that the involvement still happens. All right, accept it. Fighting involvement is the problem. If there is involvement up to seven, up to six, accept it!

Ashwin: Can I confess something else?

Ramesh: Please.

Ashwin: Earlier when I first came there was a sense of reverence for you as a person, now though there is gratitude to you as a person. I don't feel any dependency. In a sense that there is a gratitude for what you have done...

Ramesh: Gratitude arises! Gratitude arises, but Ashwin is not sure that he feels gratitude to Ramesh. Fine. Congratulations! Gratitude arises, but Ashwin finds that, personally, he does not feel any gratitude personally to Ramesh. I say, 'Congratulations'.

Ashwin: No, gratitude to a person is there. What I mean is, I don't feel the dependency in the sense that, you know, for the past few years I had this impression that there was a certain sort of dependency on a person, not to the teaching but to the person as Ramesh. Now I don't feel that dependency on the person.

Ramesh: Good. I honestly say, 'Good, congratulations!' I, myself, truly feel that I am not using the words: the teaching is only happening through me and I am not giving lectures. I mean, I myself feel it, so why shouldn't you also feel it? Therefore, I keep repeating, you cannot prevent gratitude from arising. Even if there is a personal feeling of gratitude, let it be personal. If it is not personal, let it not be personal. Why get involved in it whether it is personal or not? Why get involved in it? If it is personal, let it be personal until it disappears. If it disappears, don't wonder why. 'I want it back!', that is the problem. Whatever happens, personal or otherwise, it is there, accept it.

Ashwin: Thank you.

ૐ

Ramesh: Ok. Yes, Inge?

Inge: I just wondered about the talking. When you say about the talking, you said the talking happens. There is no thought coming into your mind first?

Ramesh: Oh no, that is the point. If thought came and I use those thoughts to say something it will be mine, my talking based on my thinking.

Inge: So, actually when you talk you respond to what you hear.

Ramesh: Yes, totally spontaneously and, therefore, I say, 'I better be careful', but I can't!

Inge: (Laughing) Because I have had experience of that. That talking happens without even having thought about what I was going to say and, actually, the things that I need to say come out much better.

Ramesh: Much better! Yes! You see, much better! That is precisely what the dancer Nijinsky has gone on record to say – 'Nijinsky dances best when Nijinsky is not there.' Everyone does everything better when everyone is not there. When something is spontaneous, whatever it is – you are playing tennis, your best game of tennis will be when you are not there. Playing tennis happens. Anything that you do, spontaneous happening is always the best. Then what happens is, 'How can I make my *doing* spontaneous?' *(Laughing)*

Inge: This you can't, you can't do. You can say, 'Ok, I need to do this and this and this today', in my work and if I get hooked on these things that I need to cover then it is gone, I can't do it.

Ramesh: What you are saying is, 'Should I or should I not plan for the day?' Sure. Plan for the day but whether the plan happens or not is not in your control. You see it everyday, therefore, there is nothing to prevent you from making the plan and satisfying yourself in the moment, but whether it works or not you can only know during the day. If it works, fine and if it doesn't work, fine.

Inge: Thank you.

૮ઇ

Ramesh: Ok. Yes, Ben?

Ben: It is for the purpose of some greater clarity and accuracy. There appear to be five components in life, one is pure subjectivity as such, and for me pure subjectivity rings better than Consciousness.

Ramesh: Fine, but then Ben can know nothing about pure

subjectivity, except as a concept. That is all. So, your concept now is, your understanding is, there has to be a Source from which everything in the manifestation has come about and since there is a manifestation, that manifestation has functioning which is life as we know it. So, once we have accepted that what is happening has not happened by coincidence, it is not some God playing dice with the universe, that there is a Source from which everything has emerged and whatever is happening to anybody, to any three-dimensional object in this manifestation, has to happen according to a Cosmic Law.

Having understood that, having being able to accept totally there is a Source from which this manifestation has happened and the functioning of this manifestation every moment depends on a Cosmic Law, having understood that, where is the need of remembering the Source? Having once accepted this, where is the question of remembering the Source? Then your only concern is with life as it happens and in life as it happens, if I am able to accept that life as it happens is the functioning of manifestation, nothing can happen unless it is according to the Cosmic Law, no question of the Source, do you see? No question of pure subjectivity.

If there is no pure subjectivity then what is the subject-object relationship? There is no subject-object relationship in pure subjectivity. But manifestation having happened and the functioning of manifestation is happening which is life as we know it. In duality, life happens because the individual having totally accepted everyone is responsible for his or her own actions, there is a continuous existence of subject-object relationship and in the subject-object relationship the basis is blaming someone or giving credit to someone. That is the subject-object relationship. But with the understanding 'no one is a doer' and you can't blame anybody, that total acceptance removes the basic earlier mistake that somebody is doing something to someone. That basis of subject-object relationship in life gets removed.

So, with this understanding, nothing can happen unless it is according to the Cosmic Law, so the happening of it, whether it happens through A, B, C or D is irrelevant. If I am going to be hurt, I am going to be hurt because I am supposed to be hurt according to the Cosmic Law. Whether the action, the deed that hurts me, happens through A, B, C, or D... irrelevant! Once I have accepted that if I am not going to be hurt, if it was not my destiny according to the Cosmic Law to be hurt, no power on earth can hurt me! That is the understanding! Therefore, there is no subject-object relationship; some subject hurting an object. When the subject-object relationship, which is the basis of life, is removed then you accept everything that happens as a happening which could not have not happened. Having accepted every event, every happening, as something which could not have not happened, the question of blaming someone or giving credit to someone simply does not arise.

Ben: *If I can come back to a concept...*

Ramesh: Sure, sure.

Ben: *The way I see it, there is the Source, pure subjectivity as such, there is a form, which is phenomenon, then there is pure subjectivity associated with the form.*

Ramesh: No, no.

Ben: *Isn't that what gives sentience to a sentient being?*

Ramesh: No. Sentient being sentient, he has not achieved sentience. So, sentience is something which had to be given to a sentient being so that the senses in that sentient being can function.

Ben: *So isn't that sentience...?*

Ramesh: Yes, Consciousness. Yes, sure.

Ben: *So, it is pure subjectivity. It is an impersonal 'I am'.*

Ramesh: Yes. I wouldn't call it pure subjectivity; it is impure subjectivity that has objectivized itself. The pure subject has become subject-object. *Shiva** has become *Shiva-Shakti*.**

Ben: *Even though it is impersonal consciousness, impersonal subjectivity...*

Ramesh: Then pure subjectivity can only be in noumenality, not in phenomenality. Therefore, the moment we are talking of phenomenality we must forget pure subjectivity. The moment we are talking about anything in life, we are talking about something happening in phenomenality and pure subjectivity cannot exist in phenomenality. Why? Because the basis of phenomenality is duality; existence of both interconnected opposites of whatever kind.

Ben: *So, it would be accurate then to use your phrase impure subjectivity?*

Ramesh: Why? Leave subjectivity alone and accept that the basis of life and living and functioning of manifestation is duality! Duality of every possible conceivable kind, beginning with male and female, beautiful and ugly.

Ben: *Because you have used the phrase pseudo-subject referring to the ego, so that is the counterpart of what?*

Ramesh: Pseudo-subject is not the impersonal subject. 'I am' is impersonal. 'I am', the impersonal awareness of existing. Pseudo-

---

*Shiva – *Consciousness unmanifest; when manifest he is portrayed as the male energy of duality.*
***Shiva-Shakti: Male-Female energy.*
Shakti – *Power, energy, capacity in the totality of manifestation; Shakti is portrayed as the female energy of duality, Shiva-Shakti; she is deified with the name of Parvati, as wife of Shiva.*

subject because there can be only one subject: subjectivity. So 'pseudo-subject' means having an object, a relationship with an object. 'Pseudo-subject' is a subject which truly doesn't exist, but which exists only when the object is there. The basis of phenomenality is subject-object relationship.

Ben: All right. Coming back to action. For action to happen through form, is ego necessary? Even ego without doership?

Ramesh: Who will live his life?

Ben: The subjectivity living, acting through the form.

Ramesh: Through the form, as what? Pure subjectivity, functioning through a particular form as a separate entity. Whoever lives his life, call it subjectivity or whatever you call it, has to live his life as a separate entity doing whatever he is supposed to do, tailor, cobbler, doctor, lawyer, banker. Whoever it is, has to live his life and carry on his profession or occupation as a separate entity.

Ben: Because in the case of the Sage, the example you have used is that it is like a burnt rope*, which means that it is ineffectual, it can't be used to do anything.

Ramesh: He continues to live his life as a separate entity but without the sense of personal doership. He continues to live his life as a separate entity and enjoys the pleasure when it arises. And who is enjoying? Ben is enjoying! You are having a very good meal; Ben knows that 'he' is enjoying the feast, not pure subjectivity! So, Ben as a separate entity enjoys the pleasure of the moment or pain in the moment *as a separate entity!* But, if somebody hurts him, the Understanding is 'no one' has hurt him,

---

* *The ego of the Sage is without any sting because the sense of personal doership has been annihilated. In the words of Ramana Maharshi (the great jnani Sage of Arunachala), the ego of the Sage is like the 'remnants of a burnt rope' – absolutely helpless and harmless.*

he is not truly the object of any subject, even if the subject thinks he is a subject and you are the object. Even if the subject thinks he hates you and loves to cause you some harm, knowing that no one is a doer, the subject-object relationship 'gets down' and you accept every happening, not as someone doing something to someone, but as a happening which could not have not happened.

Ben: Yes, hurting happened.

Ramesh: Hurting happens according to a Cosmic Law and through which body-mind organism the action happens which hurts me is irrelevant! It had to happen to hurt me. Why? Because of my destiny, according to the Cosmic Law. So, whether it happens through A, B, C or D is irrelevant. Therefore, the question of blaming someone, hating someone, simply does not arise but I still have to function in life as a separate entity accepting the hurt. Accepting the pleasure of the moment, enjoying the pleasure or accepting the hurt of the moment and doing whatever I can do in the moment to assuage the hurt, the pain. If I have a headache, I take some aspirin. 'I' take an aspirin. 'I' as Ramesh, as a separate entity, have to take an aspirin. If Ben takes an aspirin it is not going to help me. As a separate entity, if Ben takes the aspirin it is not going to help me. If I am hungry, I have to eat. Therefore, I have to live as a separate entity! No question about it, but living as a separate entity I shall never be uncomfortable with myself for having done something, or uncomfortable with anybody for his or her doing something.

Ben: Changing to identification?

Ramesh: Yes.

Ben: There are two lines of thinking here. One is that which identifies with form, so one line of thinking is that it is the ego that identifies.

Ramesh: No. Consciousness identifies itself with a particular name and form as a separate entity. Consciousness, for life to happen, has to identify itself with a particular name and form as a separate entity. Pure Consciousness, impersonal Consciousness becomes personal Consciousness, identified Consciousness by identifying itself with a particular name and form as a separate entity. And that separate entity remains until the body-mind organism is dead, but with the total Understanding, the Understanding is: 'I live my life as a separate entity' so you may say in the case of a Sage, there is separation.

Another misunderstanding: 'A Sage feels no separation', isn't it? 'Self-realization, enlightenment means no separation' and yet a Sage, even after he has become a Sage, has to live his life as a separate entity. The Sage who truly accepted this, Ramana Maharshi, was never afraid of the words 'me', 'mine', 'my loin-cloth', 'my towel', 'my food', so the Sage is never afraid of using 'me' and 'mine' as a separate entity. Of course, if there is separation then in what sense is there no separation? In the sense that the Sage has been truly able to accept totally 'no one does anything' and, therefore, all the separate entities are separate instruments, separate robots, through which the same energy functions and brings about at any moment, at any place, precisely *that* which was supposed to be brought about according to the Cosmic Law. The Sage having accepted that each separate entity is no more than a separate instrument through which the *same* energy functions, there is no separation.

Ben: *So that same energy is the subjectivity?*

Ramesh: Yes. The same subjectivity operating in phenomenality as energy.

Ben: *And the last one, about the game of life, what is called Lila**.

---

*Lila – In Hinduism, the play or game of God; the totality of manifestation looked upon as the Divine play; manifestation.

So, the identification as a separate entity and then the sense of doership...

Ramesh: Yes.

Ben: So the awakening is the converse of this movement.

Ramesh: That is correct. Consciousness identifies itself with a particular name and form as an individual doer. Self-realization is the acceptance 'no one can be a doer!'

Ben: So it is not the ego that gets free, it is the subjectivity.

Ramesh: No, subjectivity makes... freedom. Pure subjectivity gives freedom to the ego who had earlier thought, because of the divine hypnosis, that he was in bondage. The bondage of doership. So, pure subjectivity removes the sense of personal doership in an ego and the ego then is free. Free of the bondage of shame and guilt, hatred and malice. It is the ego that is the seeker, it is the ego who gets the understanding 'no one is a doer.' It is the ego who is freed from this burden of doership and, thereafter, becomes like the remnants of a burnt rope. The shape is still there, the individual entity still there, but in the absence of subject-object relationship that separate entity is harmless.

Ben: So this quote in your book, 'Pointers to Nisargadatta Maharaj' on page 129, it goes: 'So long as the body exists you are this conscious presence, the perceiving principle, when the body dies you are the absolute awareness into which the temporal consciousness merges.'

Ramesh: Therefore, the identification was just removed. Identification as a separate entity was just removed. When the body is dead all that can be is Consciousness.

Ben: So this phrase 'Conscious presence, the perceiving principle' is identified Consciousness?

Ramesh: The perceiving principle is not. The perceiving principle is Consciousness or sentience functioning through every body-mind organism, and producing that which is supposed to be produced through that body-mind organism according to a Cosmic Law.

Ben: So the second 'you'?

Ramesh: The second 'you' is the one who thought he was an individual. Now, since the body dies there is no individual. When the body dies there is no individual separate entity, therefore, what remains? What remains is the one which is always there. In other words, the river flows into the ocean... what has happened to the river? The river has become the ocean. The entity has become pure subjectivity. Truly, more accurately, the river is no longer a river. The identified entity is no longer an identified entity. Therefore, what remains is the ocean, what remains is the pure subjectivity as it has always been there.

Ben: Thank you.

૩૩

Ramesh: Ok, sure. Yes! Your name is?

Christabel: My name is Christabel.

Ramesh: What part of the world are you from?

Christabel: I am actually from Australia also, but living in Bombay for the last two months and working here.

Ramesh: So, we have an Australia day today.

Christabel: Yes, it would appear.

Ramesh: Totally unarranged! Yes, Christabel?

Christabel: You have answered, for the most part, the question I came with today and that was about the doership. Before coming to Bombay I lived on a farm, which was called Lila because there is an understanding that this is a dance of life that occurs. On a farm there is life and death, the cycles are very clear when you have no control. It is easy to see that you are not the doer. The weather comes, the weather goes... very easy to see you are not the doer. I now find myself in Bombay, working, will be here for two years. I am here in a coaching and mentoring role.

Ramesh: You are here for two months or two years?

Christabel: I have been here for two months, but I will be here for two years.

Ramesh: Oh, I see, I understand. On some mission?

Christabel: I am doing organizational consulting work. Part of what I am doing here is coaching and mentoring people and, I have found for two months, I have suffered greatly because I have been the doer. I have not been able to step back, and part of the problem is this cunning ego that has read many books, and which has picked up the knowledge that work is worship, and so there is a part of me that needs to do this work with excellence and in a spiritual way, and the best possible way...

Ramesh: Christabel, do you know where the problem is?

Christabel: Tell me.

Ramesh: The problem is very simple. Christabel says 'When I do my work and I see a certain amount of success, I feel happy but it is not my work, why should I feel happy?' Isn't that specifically the problem? So when Christabel does something which is successful, Christabel is happy.

Christabel: It is the doing of the work which is the success for me. It is the doing of the work on which I place the importance.

Ramesh: Yes. So in the doing of the work, it is your own experience that sometimes it is best, sometimes it is average, sometimes not so good and there is nothing you can do about it. That is your experience. So your own experience is, Christabel always tries to do her best. Why? Because it is the nature of this person called Christabel to always do her best. The body-mind organism called Christabel is so programmed, genes plus conditioning, which makes Christabel a responsible, hard-working person who always likes to do her best. So Christabel tries to do her best but the actual experience is sometimes the best happens, very often the best doesn't happen. So when the best happens Christabel is happy. When Christabel does her best and it works, brings about success, Christabel is happy. So, the problem Christabel has is 'I do something and I am happy but I am supposed to feel that it is not 'me' doing it', you see? That is the problem.

Christabel: Yes, yes.

Ramesh: My point to you is: the arising of pleasure because of something done is not Christabel being happy, but the pleasure arising in a body-mind organism. When the eyes see something, ears hear something and the feeling there is success, there is happiness, *someone* is happy. So the happiness or pleasure that arises out of a job well done – not by 'me', it happens to be well done – pleasure arises, Christabel. Pleasure arises in a body-mind organism.

Now, if I continue to give my concept and I find Christabel truly able to respond to it and I can see the impact and I can see the happiness in Christabel's face, that will bring pleasure in this body-mind organism. Certainly, pleasure will arise in this body-mind organism but I need feel no guilt because I am happy, because I have done a good job. No, the arising of pleasure for a job well done, the arising of regret for a job that happened to be badly done, arises in the body-mind organism and the individual is not happy nor regrets. With this understanding that pleasure arises and, at the same time, knowing that it is not Christabel's work that has brought pleasure, the pleasure will be there in the instant but it will not be accompanied by pride.

Christabel: (Laughing) That is the big one!

Ramesh: You see, pleasure will arise but never the pride. The other side, regret may arise but never guilt or shame, 'Not my action', you see? So, the pleasure or the regret arises in the body-mind organism. When the ego responds to that natural action, 'I did a good job', pleasure and pride. 'I did a bad job', regret plus shame and guilt. Therefore, you often see a Sage quite happy, a Sage quite angry, but what the Sage has accepted is that in some cases anger has arisen, sometimes pleasure has arisen, and he thoroughly enjoys the pleasure, make no mistake!

Christabel: So, do you unhook the feeling of pleasure that arises in the organism from the ego taking over, making pride?

Ramesh: The ego's reaction is as a personal doer. When the personal doership is not there, the ego does not react to the pleasure with pride or regret with a sense of guilt. Therefore, the arising of the pleasure or the regret is beyond Christabel's control. Christabel witnesses pleasure arising, pleasure arises because the society gives... to Christabel, but knowing that she has not done anything then the pleasure, if anything, will be joined by a sense of amusement, 'I am being honored when it is not my work'. So, pleasure but not pride, regret but not shame or guilt, hurt but not hatred or malice for someone else's doing.

Christabel: So now... it is practically making that happen... (Laughing)

Ramesh: (*Laughing*) Just watch it happen. What I am saying is:

enjoy the pleasure! Don't try to smother it. Regret arises, don't try to smother it, express your regret.

Christabel: Yes.

ॐ

Ramesh: Yes, please?

(French woman asks a question via an interpreter.)

Interpreter: She would like to know how you live the experience of Self, with the big S.

Ramesh: I said: if there is pleasure, I enjoy the pleasure. If there is pain, I do something to reduce it. If I have a headache, I take an aspirin.

Interpreter: That is it. Thank you.

Ramesh: Ok. Most welcome.

Day 2

Ramesh: Good Morning, Alex!

Alex: *Ummm... I don't know where to begin really, but... ummm... yesterday I was thinking a lot about the whole talk we had.*

Ramesh: Yes...

Alex: *And I don't think I really, sort of, opened up or came clear with my feelings about the concepts that you talk about.*

Ramesh: So, today are you going to open up?

Alex: *(Laughing) I will try.*

Ramesh: *(Laughing)* Yes, Alex, that is all one can do!

Alex: *Yeah... I certainly, ummm... there was some strange feeling within me after the talk and during the talk yesterday...*

Ramesh: I see...

Alex: *...and I could not figure out in my head what was going on. Certainly when I first came to know of your teachings...*

Ramesh: Now, tell me first, Alex, what you heard here was nothing complicated, was it?

Alex: *No, that is the thing... it was nothing complicated and there is nothing new that I heard either. But it wasn't... I don't think I... I hardly heard a word you said! I didn't want to hear a word you said.*

Ramesh: I see.

Alex: *I don't know why... it was like a battle between maybe my ego or something... it just didn't want to hear what you had to say. It was like arrogance or something. It took me a long time yesterday to actually figure out what was happening. I don't even know if that was the answer.*

Ramesh: What you mean is, you were trying to find out where the resistance was.

Alex: *Yes.*

Ramesh: There was some resistance...

Alex: *Yes.*

Ramesh: ...to what was being said.

Alex: *But there has never been a resistance before. There is me stepping into this room and there is resistance when I never had resistance to your concepts before...*

Ramesh: I see. I see.

Alex: *...which I found very peculiar. I don't know why... why has that happened?*

Ramesh: Yes. But tell me what do you think is the core of what I have said?

Alex: Ummm... that everything just happens.

Ramesh: To go back, back to the core of what I say. What would you say is the core of what I say, Alex? The core of what I say is what the Buddha said: 'Events happen, deeds are done, and there is no individual doer thereof.' So, with the acceptance of this concept, what does Buddha say? Buddha says, 'This will lead you to enlightenment'.

Alex: Ummm... ummm...

Ramesh: 'Acceptance of this concept of non-doership will lead you to enlightenment' and, then he says, 'What is enlightenment? Enlightenment is the end of suffering.' And what is this suffering which the Buddha refers to? And my point is, the suffering which the Buddha refers to, to which enlightenment brings about the end, is clearly not the suffering which the human being must endure as an animal. The human being is first an animal which has a mind-intellect which distinguishes him from the animal. Just as the animal cannot escape suffering in this life, the human being as an animal cannot escape suffering in this life. So, Buddha didn't mean that kind of suffering which the human being must suffer as an animal. Therefore, the suffering which Buddha says enlightenment brings the end of, because of being able to accept that no one is a doer, is a suffering which the animal does not suffer. So, what is the suffering which the human being suffers...

Alex: ...doership.

Ramesh: ...and the animal doesn't? The animal doesn't have a sense of personal doership, whereas the human being has this sense of personal doership which distinguishes him, and the human being is proud! That is what distinguishes him from an animal. 'You take away my free will, you reduce me to an animal!' You see? 'Therefore, I am prepared to give up anything but not my free will!' It is this concept of free will, doership, which causes that kind of suffering, which Buddha says can end only with enlightenment, and enlightenment can happen only if you are able to accept, by God's grace, the fact of non-doership. You see?

Alex: Yeah.

Ramesh: End of suffering! So, what is the suffering? Suffering which the human being, because of the mind-intellect, creates for himself! Which the animal doesn't! Therefore, when the Buddha said 'End of suffering', it is most important for the human being to understand what kind of suffering, the end of which is promised by Buddha. That suffering is not day-to-day suffering which the animal suffers, but the suffering which the mind-intellect human being has created for himself because of thinking he is the doer, and everybody else is a doer. You see, Alex? That is the core of what I am saying. Simple enough, isn't it?

Alex: Very.

Ramesh: So, where is the problem?

(Laughter in the room...)

Alex: (Laughing) I was just... I was just reacting. Sort of a reaction.

Ramesh: Yes.

Alex: I don't know where to... well... I know where to go next... but ummm...

Ramesh: So, the core of what I am saying, where can the resistance come from?

Alex: From my ego, from my doership.

Ramesh: The ego simply is not prepared to give up its sense of personal doership without the biggest fight it has ever had!

Alex: Certainly it was happening yesterday.

Ramesh: You felt you didn't want to give up the sense of personal doership... free will?

Alex: I was having a battle with free will yesterday in my head... umm... thinking a lot about it. And how little free will, I thought I had in the past, anyway.

Ramesh: And another point I make is, 'the human sense of free will and independent entity who can do whatever it wants'... that is the important thing! So now my point is, from our own experience, let us find out what is the big deal about this free will that I have. What is this free will? What does the free will amount to? From my own experience, I know it is my free will according to which I choose what I want in life. So, therefore, 'I' choose what 'I' want in my life. Then, according to my own free will, I decide how I shall get it and in deciding that I will also have decided, 'I want it. If anyone comes in my way, I will try to smash him out of my way!' Or I say, because of my genes, 'I simply can't do it, I can only make a plan which will appeal to my consciousness. I cannot choose a plan which will hurt others.' So which one you will decide, with consciousness or without consciousness, is truly not your choice. Even that depends on your genes. You see? So, having decided from my own choice the plan according to which I plan to get what I want, then the only remaining thing is I put in my best efforts. So, 'I' choose what I want. 'I' make the plan. And 'I' put in my best effort, beyond that where does my free will take me? That is all. My free will ends when I decide what I want and put in my best efforts. Beyond that my free will cannot function. And that is everybody's experience.

Sometimes my best efforts produce the best results. Sometimes my best efforts do not produce even ordinarily good results. That, sometimes, is my experience... for some reason or the other – ill health, accident or whatever. Sometimes, for some reason beyond my control, I am not able to put in my best efforts and yet the results are fantastic. Do you see what I mean?

Alex: Yeah.

Ramesh: Therefore, if life tells me very clearly, as I sow, so I reap, it is not correct. My life tells me that. So, on this big deal about free will, what I am saying is, if from our own experience, if we analyze, we have to come to the conclusion: 'I choose what I want. I put in my best efforts', that is where my free will ends. Then, next point is, how do I choose what I want? I have to use my intellect, isn't it? And if I am not gifted with super-intellect, I can only use my moderate intellect. So, my free will to choose depends on the intellect which God has given me. I did not choose my intellect out of my free will. You see?

Alex: Yeah.

Ramesh: And the extent of effort that I am going to put in also depends truly on my physical and other assets which God has given me. Therefore, my ordinary efforts will often be much better than someone else's best efforts. And, sometimes, my best efforts may not come anywhere near someone else's best efforts. So, considering all this, what does the free will really amount to?!? Nothing!

(Laughter in the room.)

Ramesh: You see? Having chosen what I want, having put in my best efforts, that is it! After that my free will is hopeless. Helpless. So, if we analyze from our own experience, we come to the conclusion that free will is not what it is boasted about. It has great limitations. So, having come to this conclusion, what do I do? Having come to this conclusion, the core point is: With this understanding, I truly don't have any free will and, even if I think I have free will, it can take me only to the border. Beyond this border it has never been in anybody's control, because so many diverse factors come into operation.

So, with this understanding, how does Alex live his life? Very simple; with this understanding, Alex chooses whatever he thinks he wants and Alex accepts that, because of the limitation of his intellect, what he chooses may not be considered by many others to be a very good choice.

First, you accept that your choice may not be the best. Second, you decide that 'my genes prevent me from taking the direct route, which is to smash everything before me, I can't do that!' so knowing that, you can only put in such efforts as your genes and conditioning let you put. Having put in your best efforts, now knowing that the results are *not* in your control, what happens? Then you stop blaming yourself for what has happened in the past, you stop blaming yourself for not being able to put in efforts as good as the other man, and you stop yourself from fretting about the future which has never been in anyone's hands ever!

So, what does Alex do? Alex does whatever he thinks he should do in the moment. And having done it, Alex doesn't get frustrated. 'What do I do?' You do whatever you think you should do in a present moment. No problem. Where does the problem come in? The problem comes in when 'I want to do better than anybody else!' That is where the problem comes in. I can't, every time, do better than others. All I can do is to do what I am programmed, designed and conditioned to do. It may not be as good as some of the others, but it may be better than many of the others.

So, what this understanding leads to is the acceptance of What Is. And, therefore, when this understanding is total and the person is considered a wise man, what does the wise man know, immediately, as soon as he gets this understanding in total?

First thing he knows is that, in his own case, his own programming, all that his physical assets amount to are several good points and quite a few bad points. Plus points, minus points. Positive points, negative points. And there is nothing he can do about it.

But if someone thinks he can do something about it, let him do it! Read books on self-improvement! But if I expect those books to do something for me and they don't, I feel frustrated! So, if I don't want frustration I read self-improvement books without expecting particular results. So, having done my self-improvement course, then my physical and mental assets are at their best, so what do I do? I use those assets the best way I can, knowing that compared to others... I simply cannot compare. With this understanding, therefore, no problem arises! I do what I think I should do to the best of my abilities and then leave the results to whatever then happens, because the understanding is, what effort I am going to put in depends on what the Cosmic Law expects me to do. And, the results also are, precisely, what I am supposed to have according to a Cosmic Law.

So, with this understanding, Alex, my only point is; all that will happen is that you will be living a simpler life, not getting complicated with expectations and to that extent you will have less frustration in life, more composure, more harmony and peace. That is all, according to my concept, that enlightenment can do for you. The Buddha says, 'Being able to accept life as it happens, without creating expectations, is enlightenment.' And enlightenment, therefore, is this acceptance of non-doership and acceptance of whatever is in the moment. The acceptance is, 'I have what has been given to me, some plus points and some minus points.' The same applies to everybody in the world. No one has had any control over his physical and mental assets. So, with this understanding, I don't expect myself to do any better than I am, I don't expect Alex to be any better than what he is designed to be. So, the first thing that happens when this understanding is complete, is I realize my own limitations and

I realize that everybody has his own limitations! Which means I do not ever expect to be a perfect human being, and I do not expect anyone else to be a perfect human being either! That is all, according to me. This is also precisely what the Buddha says.

Considering myself the doer, considering that I have free will and considering everybody else has the same thing – and, therefore, everybody is responsible for his work – means suffering. And that is the suffering which ends when I am able to accept no one is a doer! No one could have been better than what he is. No one could have been worse than what he is. He is what he is! That is all it amounts to.

Alex: Certainly clear.

Ramesh: (*Laughing*)

Alex: Whether it sinks in or not... I don't know.

Ramesh: Any particular question arose in your mind yesterday, Alex?

Alex: No, I was just simply battling, I think, with free will and my ego and what happened here yesterday. It was just a kind of, umm... a bit of a numbness really.

Ramesh: (*Laughing*) Numbness... yes.

Alex: Yeah. I didn't really come up with any questions.

Ramesh: I see.

Alex: So, I think I just wanted to tell you that was weird... what was going on yesterday. Because it was the first experience of...

Ramesh: Now tell me, what you heard yesterday and today,

do you think it will present a problem for Alex to live his life from now on?

Alex: No, it is... I think... umm... from the first moment, no, not the first moment, when I first started reading your concepts, I did notice a change in my life... it has been simpler since then.

Ramesh: You mean even the intellectual acceptance of this concept did something to your life? Did you say?..

Alex: Yeah, I was, I was living a bit more in the moment. Umm...

Ramesh: That is a technical statement. (*Laughing*) 'I have been living more in the moment', (*Laughing*)... what does it mean?

Alex: I wasn't thinking so much about...

Ramesh: Ah! About the past or the future!

Alex: Yeah.

Ramesh: Therefore, you didn't fret about the past which is dead. Nor about the future which hasn't happened yet.

Alex: Although it did come up. But it was less, it was less.

Ramesh: Yes.

Alex: So, there was a little bit less...

Ramesh: But tell me, Alex, if you are able to accept this totally, does it mean that you don't go into the past at all?

Alex: No, you have to.

Ramesh: How can you not?

Alex: Yeah.

Ramesh: If you are doing a job in the instant, for e.g. a surgeon has a body before him, and it is very important that he chooses the right place to make an incision. He has to decide where do I make the incision. What can he do except go back into his own experience in the past and then decide the best place to make the incision. So, for that, he has to go into the past!

Therefore, what I am saying is, there are two aspects of the mind. One is, what I call, the *working mind*. The *working mind* functions only in the present moment. The *working mind* decides where to make the incision for the surgeon. For that reason, the *working mind* of the surgeon has to go back into his past experience. But having learned from the past experience, the *working mind* stops in the present moment. Having decided where to make the incision, the *working mind* doesn't go into the past. But the other aspect, the *thinking mind*, is always in the past or the future, never in the present moment. Therefore, what happens in the case of an ordinary person is, while the *working mind* is trying to do a job to the best of its ability, the *thinking mind* keeps interrupting the *working mind*. Warning him, 'What would happen if you fail?'. To a surgeon, for instance, it says, 'Do you know who you are operating on? It is a minister's son! Do you know what is going to happen if you fail?' That kind of a thing. But the *working mind* is not concerned.

Therefore, my concept, Alex, is, the extent to which any ordinary person is successful in his career, whatever the career, my concept is, the extent to which he is successful or not depends on the extent to which the *thinking mind* interrupts the *working mind*. If the person is lucky enough to be able to concentrate his *working mind* on the job that is being done and not have the *thinking mind* interfere, he will be successful. Therefore, in life, it is our experience anywhere, that the most successful person in any sphere is not necessarily the best one. Not the best one according to intellect, qualifications or anything. Someone must necessarily have the ability, the qualifications – that goes without saying – but among the many who have those qualifications, what I am saying is, everybody's experience is such that, the one who succeeds is not necessarily the best qualified, but someone who is lucky enough to have the *thinking mind* interrupting his *working mind* much less than the others. You see? This is precisely what the dancer Nijinsky means, when he says, 'Nijinsky dances best when Nijinsky is not there.'

And another instance in which I could see the same happening, was some three, four years ago. Are you interested in tennis?

Alex: Yes.

Ramesh: Did you see that match three years ago, between Pete Sampras, the champion, and the Russian lad, 19 years old? Pete Sampras, number one, and his opponent, ranked 246 or something like that. No competition. You see? I don't know, but the betting must have been 'Name your odds', for the challenger to be a winner, 'Name your odds!', and yet do you know the challenger won, he beat the champion and the champion was dazed. So, at the end of the match the media people went to him and they asked, 'Pete, how did you manage to lose it?' So, Pete is supposed to have said, 'Today no tennis player in the world could have beaten the Russian lad.'

Then they went to the Russian lad, 'How did you manage to beat him? Did you have a plan? Did you have a plan on how to beat this champion?' He said, 'No. I decided at the very beginning that it would be stupid to expect to beat the champion, therefore, I never hoped to beat the champion, therefore, I had to make some plan'. So he decided on the plan, 'I plan to leave the match to itself and be concerned only with returning every shot that comes to me'. So, he didn't think of the match, he didn't think of the set, he didn't think of the game in the set, all he was concerned with was returning the shot, which came to him.

With that, Sampras hit a shot which he thought was a definite, a killer! And he didn't expect the shot to come back. The *thinking mind* said, 'You can relax' and Pete relaxed. The Russian went at it and sent it back. So many times you could see Pete standing there, gaping. So, all that the Russian lad thought was, 'I shall return every ball that comes to me' and he did. So, the Russian lad was able to keep his *thinking mind* away from his *working mind* and the job for the *working mind* was simple, 'Return the shot!' That is all. You see what I mean?

Therefore, acceptance does not mean *not* doing whatever is needed to be done in the present moment. Acceptance of What Is does *not* mean merely sitting back and watching something happening, but doing whatever is necessary to be done in the moment. Therefore, the question is, with the understanding that no one is a doer, 'how do I live my life?' Very simple. At any moment, do whatever you think you have to do! Forget the rest. As simple as that. Simple in theory, not so simple to practice.

Alex: I don't know if I have any more questions.

Ramesh: So, you don't have any more questions?

Alex: I don't think so.

Ramesh: Fine. Will you pass on the mike to our friend? If you can put it on, so much the better. Yes. Excellent. Excellent. That is it. Yes sir, your name is?

George: My name is George.

Ramesh: George, yes. Which part of the world are you from?

George: I am from Washington State in the United States.

Ramesh: I see. And what do you do in the United States?

George: *I am a chiropractor.*

Ramesh: Chiropractor. I see, I see. Practicing on your own or part of an establishment?

George: *On my own.*

Ramesh: On your own. I see. I see. And how long do you think you have been a seeker, George? Would you consider yourself a spiritual seeker?

George: *Yes. Ummm... I would say, probably since I was a child.*

Ramesh: Ah! In fact what you say is, ever since you were a child certain questions bothered you, which didn't bother other children. Would that be it?

George: *I don't know. I don't know if they bothered other children or not. But for me, ummm... I had questions...*

Ramesh: I see. I see. What sort of questions, George?

George: *Ummm...*

Ramesh: Who am I? What am I doing in this world? That kind of a thing?

George: *Yeah and maybe questions to the religion that I was raised in.*

Ramesh: What was that? Catholic?

George: *Fundamentalist, Protestant upbringing.*

Ramesh: I see. So, as a child do you remember what kind of

problems, questions bothered you as a Christian? You said religion bothered you, so what kind of questions bothered you then?

George: I remember as a child, thinking, you know reading the stories in the New Testament about the Pharisees being classed as the bad guys and thinking, 'well, it seems like we are the Pharisees.' You know, in the church, you know, a particular culture it seemed... There was something that came at me, it seems like this group that I belong to is the Pharisees. I remember quite as a young child thinking that.

Ramesh: You didn't put those questions to your priest? You didn't dare to?

George: (Laughing) Yeah, I kept those more quiet.

Ramesh: I see. Anytime the question came you said 'Shut up!' (*Laughing*).

George: Yeah.

Ramesh: So, how long has your seeking been more active, George?

George: I think since my teen years. Maybe about seventeen, eighteen.

Ramesh: When you were seventeen, eighteen?

George: Yeah.

Ramesh: What course did that seeking take, George? What kind of reading did you do? What kind of people did you go to?

George: Ummm... I remember just having a philosophy of loving, learning and living. That was sort of my philosophy at that time, how I articulated what I... just exploring what interested me.

Ramesh: But what reading did that exploring take you to? Didn't you do any reading?

George: *Yes. Ummm...*

Ramesh: What kind of reading? Gurdjieff, Ouspensky? J. Krishnamurti?

George: *More Taoist thought.*

Ramesh: Oh, really! I see. So, you had that grace in the first place? To go to Tao.

George: *I've always loved that. Yeah.*

Ramesh: I see.

George: *A lot of writers in the Catholic tradition. Kind of integrating psychology and religion. That sort of exploration. But sort of whatever interests me; I just sort of follow that call.*

Ramesh: So, it's been quite a few years since you have been a spiritual seeker. Can you tell me, George, what it is that you have been seeking? What did you expect to get at the end of that seeking? Enlightenment? Self-realization?

George: *Just understanding, having some sort of a way of understanding life, richness of, of... feeling my own experience.*

Ramesh: A sense of fulfillment you would say?

George: *Connection. A sense of connection. A sense of, maybe, belonging at some level to what is. Ummm... yeah.*

Ramesh: I see. Would you say, 'Being one with the Source?', 'Being one with God?' so that you don't feel different from anything else in the world. 'Being one with God', would that be one?

George: I don't know. I don't know. Maybe that is all scary. Ummm...

Ramesh: All right. Let me put it this way, whatever it is that George has been seeking. What did George expect the fulfillment of that seeking to do for George, for the rest of his life? What do you expect that which you were seeking to do for you, for the rest of your life that you didn't have before? See what I mean?

George: Yeah. Yeah. I think maybe just a greater sense of comfort.

Ramesh: Yes, I see, a greater sense of comfort. What you truly mean, I think, George, is the sense of not being uncomfortable with yourself, not being uncomfortable with others.

George: Right.

Ramesh: I quite agree. Ultimately what it comes down to is, what anybody is seeking, assuming, of course, I keep repeating, that you have been lucky enough to be in life with a certain amount of comfort. In other words, that you are not below the poverty line. If I ask someone below the poverty line, 'What do you want most in life?', the answer has to be, 'Sufficient money to have food, clothing and shelter'. Therefore, I am not talking on this subject to anyone below the poverty line. I am talking to someone who is reasonably comfortable in life. Reasonably comfortable or very comfortable in life. To such a person, who is reasonably comfortable in life and, even better off, what does he want most in life? You see what I mean?

George: Yeah.

Ramesh: What does a spiritual seeker, who is reasonably

comfortable in life, is not below the poverty line, what does he want most in life?

George: *You are asking me?*

Ramesh: Yes. What do you say?

George: *For myself, I think just a sense of connection. A sense of...*

Ramesh: My point is, George, that is precisely what everyone wants, whether he knows it or not. As simple as that. 'I want to be truly comfortable with myself and I cannot be truly comfortable with myself if I am not comfortable with the others!' Therefore, what I want is to be truly comfortable with myself and with the others. Which again means, what is the standard of being comfortable with myself? Say that in the negative: 'I don't ever want to hate myself for anything. I don't want to be able to hate someone else.' Therefore, if I am able not to hate myself at any time or to hate anyone else, then I am comfortable with myself! Then, I am never uncomfortable with myself and I am never uncomfortable with the others. Then the question is, what makes me truly uncomfortable with myself?

George: *Judging?*

Ramesh: Yes. Judgment of what, George? My concept is, judgment of what I did to someone or what I did not do for someone that I could have done. A thought of something I did, which I should not have done, and something I didn't do for someone that I could have done. So that, anytime I have that feeling of never being comfortable with anybody... anytime I had that feeling of being truly comfortable, a thought from the past shatters that feeling of being comfortable. What is the thought? The thought, which is a judgment, of what I did to someone or something that I did not do for someone that I could have done. See what I mean? Any time I have that feeling of comfort, it is demolished if a thought happens – if a thought happens I have no control over that – about what I did or did not do, my feeling of comfort is shattered! Similarly, a thought of someone else who did to me what he shouldn't have done or did not do for me what he could have done. Similarly, the places have changed. Then, any thought of that reminds me that I have hated that person ever since that happened.

In other words, my point is, how can I always remain never uncomfortable with myself nor with the other? Only if I am able to accept – no one does anything! Only if I am able to accept, totally, the basic principle of every religion. The Bible says, 'Thy will be done'. What does it mean? A simple 'Thy will be done' simply means, without any scope for misunderstanding, whatever happens can only happen if it is God's Will otherwise it cannot happen. Something happens, I accept that it is God's Will but what happens now? What happens now is, instead of accepting whatever is as God's Will I judge it as good or bad. And if I judge it as bad, I ask God, 'God, you are supposed to be all-merciful, why are you doing this? Why are you creating handicapped children?' Therefore, expecting God to do something only good I become uncomfortable with myself. If I am able to accept that whatever happens, happens according to a Cosmic Law, a Cosmic Law according to which, ever since time began every little thing happens strictly according to that Cosmic Law. An impersonal Cosmic Law. Then, I stop judging people. I stop judging myself and I stop judging others. And that is all that is truly necessary to make me always comfortable with myself, and never uncomfortable with the others.

That is the core of what I am saying: Only if we are able to accept totally the basic principle in every religion, the Bible says: 'Thy will be done'. The Koran, I think, says: 'Inshallah', Inshallah – God Willing. The average Muslim, after almost every other sentence says, 'Inshallah'. 'Are you going somewhere tomorrow?' 'Yes, I am looking forward to it, Inshallah!' The Hindu religion,

George, says, 'Thou art the doer, Thou art the experiencer. Thou art the speaker, Thou art the listener'. So what the Hindu religion says is, George may think, 'Ramesh speaks, George listens' or 'George speaks, Ramesh listens' but it is not true. It may seem like that but what is really happening is the Primal Energy functioning through two human body-mind instruments, the Primal Energy produces the talking in one, the listening in the other. The Primal Energy produces the talking and the Primal Energy produces the listening. So, the talking and the listening is a happening brought about by the Primal Energy through two different body-mind organisms. You see? So, the whole basis or the basic principle in every religion is, no human being is truly the doer of any actions. Actions happen! And that is precisely what the Buddha came to, that is precisely the conclusion the Buddha came to after a lot of suffering because of other concepts. Only when he accepted this concept, 'Events happen, deeds are done, there is no individual doer thereof', did his thinking stop. Events happen, deeds are done, there is no individual doer thereof.

George: *But we make a choice of our will to accept and, in that sense, to make the shift that you are talking about we have to consciously say, 'I accept' and isn't that a use of free will? A choice? Umm...*

Ramesh: Now, tell me, George, three people are listening. One person says, at the end of the talk, 'Maybe you are right'. Another person says, 'I accept it totally!' The third person says, 'It is all rubbish! How can life function if every human being is not held responsible for his or her actions? Life cannot happen. With this theory that the human being has no free will, life cannot function!' See what I mean? All three, they think they have chosen; one to reject it, another to accept it totally, and one says, 'Maybe'. So, is it truly their choice? Is it truly the individual's choice?

George: *From their perspective, it is.*

Ramesh: From 'their' perspective! And what is that perspective,

George? That is my point. What is the perspective from which each person thinks he is using his free will? In other words, what is the basis on which the individual decides according to his free will? What is the basis? The basis according to my concept is, the genes in this body-mind organism and the up to date conditioning. You had no choice, George, about being born to particular parents; therefore, George had no control over the genes in this human object. And as you know, more and more research has been coming out with the conclusion that whatever the human being does, good, bad or indifferent, can be traced to his genes.

George: *Do you think genetics is God? Is that what you are saying?*

Ramesh: No, my point is, your genes are what they are. You had no choice about those genes!

George: *I am just asking a question...*

Ramesh: Wait a minute. There is no free will about your genes...

George: *Right.*

Ramesh: ...then what I am saying is, whatever you base your decision on truly depends on two things: Your genes plus your up to date conditioning over which you had no control. Just as you had no control over being born to particular parents, George had no control over being born to particular parents in a particular geographical environment, and in a particular social environment in that geographical environment. And in that social and geographical environment this body-mind organism, called George, received his conditioning from day one! Conditioning at home, conditioning in society, conditioning in school, conditioning in church or temple. 'This is good, that is bad, you must do this, you must not do that'. 'This is good, that is bad! You must choose this, you must not choose that!' 'You must *choose* this, you must not *choose* that!' Based on these genes plus conditioning, whatever George decides to do out of his 'free will' can only depend on his genes over which he had no control and the up to date conditioning over which also, truly, George has no control.

So, what is this free will? On what basis do I, using my free will, make a choice? It cannot be other then my genes and my up to date conditioning, over which I had no control!

George: *Seems like there is...*

Ramesh: One moment. Yes Ma'am? (*Responding to a woman who had put her hand up*)

Martha: *Thank you. I wanted to say that I feel that if, when I act, I act with my full consciousness and I am aware of the law of cause and effect, I am able to go beyond my genes. I find myself sort of a channel of God. Whatever it is, then I have no more genes. They are over!*

Ramesh: No, your genes... Let me tell you a story, your genes preclude you from being a homosexual. Can you prevent the genes and be a homosexual?

Martha: *Maybe. I mean I am not conditioned by my past and I don't think on the past.*

Ramesh: Therefore...

Martha: *I am very attentive to what I am doing just now, then why not?*

Ramesh: Now, wait a minute. What I am saying is, every human being is programmed in a way over which he or she had no control.

One is genes and the other is up to date conditioning. I use the word up to date, I am sorry, your name is?

Martha: Martha.

Ramesh: Martha, I use up to date conditioning because what is happening now is conditioning, make no mistake!

Martha: Yes, but let's say if my mobile phone, if I hadn't been aware that I had to switch it off, it would have sounded... so then, that is my will. My consciousness. I decided not to disturb anybody with my mobile. I mean, this is just an example for the rest of the life.

Ramesh: But you decided to switch off your mobile. 'You', 'you' decided to switch off the mobile...

Martha: Exactly, not to disturb others... so I will have the effect of no sound...

Ramesh: Wait a minute, wait a minute. The mobile was on; at a certain point Martha decided to switch off the phone. Why?

Martha: Not to disturb anyone and to be aware of what is happening here.

Ramesh: Therefore, a thought occurred...

Martha: A what?

Ramesh: A thought occurred.

Martha: An alert?

(Other people repeated: 'A thought occurred'.)

Martha: Well, or an intuition. I mean...

Ramesh: An intuitive thought but 'some thought'! I am told by physicists that what thought comes in my head, whatever thought happens to anybody, is beyond anyone's control. How does a thought happen? A thought happens and according to the physicists, out of thousands of probabilities, one probability collapses into a thought in a particular body-mind organism. When Martha responds to that thought, it is only almost half a second later. Martha responds to that thought half a second later after the thought has occurred! Therefore, Martha had absolutely no control over the thought that happened. So, here the thought happens, that 'there are other people, I don't want to disturb them' and that thought led to your action of switching off the mobile! If that thought had not happened, Martha would not have switched off the mobile.

Martha: But I want to say, that is a thought, that is consciousness. It is completely different!

Ramesh: I see (*Laughing*). The thought occurred from the Consciousness. You did not create the thought. That is what I am saying. You did not create the thought of switching off the mobile...

Martha: No, I just had the conscious, the awareness to be careful to do, and come here in the best conditions. That's it, so...

Ramesh: I see. Now, you are here.

Martha: Yes.

Ramesh: Out of your own choice?

Martha: Yes.

Ramesh: That is what you are saying, 'You are here now out of your choice!' and Martha what I am saying is, in spite of being very mindful, supposing you had felt you are in pain. You did not want to be in pain, surely! But you are in pain and that could have prevented you from being here.

Martha: If I had caught a cold because I would have been in a current... I could not have been here...

Ramesh: That is my point. Therefore, any number of things could have happened to prevent Martha from being here at this moment. They didn't! And that they didn't was not in your control, Martha!

Martha: I think so. I think so.

Ramesh: Fine, ok.

Martha: Sometimes, I mean, if you believe...

Ramesh: Sometimes. I see.

Martha: Let's say I think I control my attention and my intention. I don't control what is going to happen. So, I am not attached to what is going to happen.

Ramesh: I see.

Martha: But I control my intention and my attention. And that one is very important.

Ramesh: So, and therefore, Martha can take an intensive course in Vitamin C and prevent a cold from happening! Martha prevented a cold from happening by taking an intensive course of C Vitamin! It is in Martha's hands not to have a cold!

Martha: No, I would never take a course of C Vitamin.

Ramesh: Ok, Martha, you keep your concept of doership and I...

Martha: What?

Ramesh: Doership. Personal doership.

Martha: No, I don't feel there is no doer.

Ramesh: So, Martha believes she is the doer of all her actions.

Martha: No, if I fail it is because I am the doer. If I am a channel of divinity and fail, and I also do, it is the doer that fails. So, I have the possibility of being the doer or being the channel of the doer.

Ramesh: So, my point is, every human being is a channel, through which the Primal Energy functions. That is my concept. Every human being is no more than a channel for the Primal Energy to function and bring about whatever is supposed to be brought about, according to God's Will or according to a Cosmic Law. That is my point. Ok.

Yes. (*Talking to George*) Do you have any question on what we have covered so far?

George: Yeah, I guess I see in my own understanding and experience as somewhat of a dance.

Ramesh: Life is a flow!

George: Yes, but a dance in how I understand things... I am just... I see things in a paradox. So, whenever someone says, it is all determined, there is no choice at all, everything is determined, then a little light goes on in my head and says, 'What about the paradox, you know?' Maybe, usually there is a dance between two sides, you know, and what I hear you saying is, 'No, there is just one, one side.'

Ramesh: No. Oh no, on the contrary! The concept is that, anything at any moment in life cannot be other than the existence at the same time of two interconnected polaric opposites of every conceivable kind, beginning with male and female! Therefore, the manifestation, the functioning of which is life as we know it, the basis of it is the existence of interconnected polaric opposites at the same time, beginning, as I said, with male and female.

George: *But not choice and destiny.*

Ramesh: No, my point is, both exist! And one cannot exist without the other. Therefore, the Sage, the wise man has accepted the basis of life and its happening as the existence at any moment of both the interconnected opposites. In other words, the Sage, the moment he became a Sage, has accepted the duality of life, and has accepted that anybody living his life has to live in duality!

But with most people what happens? They keep on choosing one against the other. The average person keeps on choosing one against the other – 'only the good, not the bad'; 'only the beautiful, not the ugly' – or choosing one superior to the other. That is why the average person is unhappy and frustrated. In other words, the average man is frustrated and unhappy because he is unable to accept the basic duality of life and, therefore, he lives in dualism choosing one against the other as better or superior. Something wanted, something not wanted. So, the average person is not able to accept the duality of life, accepting that both exist, must exist at the same time. Chooses one against the other, 'always the beautiful, never the ugly', 'always the good, never the bad'. Therefore, the average person says, 'Hitler is bad, evil. Hitler should not have been there! Because of Hitler millions of Jews had to die. It cannot be the work of God, surely. The merciful God could not have brought about the deaths of millions of Jews for which Hitler is responsible'. Therefore, the average person says, 'God did not create Hitler!' Then, if God did not create Hitler, who created Hitler? 'Satan created Hitler'. So, God and

Satan! In competition! So, God is not the Source! So, the question now is, 'Who created God and Satan?' And you go back and back, 'Who created B and C?'

So, therefore, my point is, we have to accept the Source as that from which everything comes. Both the dualities. Both the interconnected opposites. In fact, God and Satan themselves are interconnected opposites. As one of the many interconnected opposites. So, if we accept the Source as one from which everything has come, then the bad and the good, the beautiful and the ugly, good and evil, all must have come from the same Source. Why? Because the interconnected opposites are the very basis of manifestation and its functioning, that we call life as we know it. Therefore, deeply, the Sage is a Sage and he lives his life accepting the duality of life, which means the next moment will bring for everybody pain or pleasure, and nobody can choose it. Whereas the ordinary person becomes frustrated because he *always* wants good health, never the sickness! *Always* the beautiful, never the ugly! *Always* good, *always* Jesus Christ and no Hitlers! And, therefore, always Christs or someone else... the American president but never Saddam Hussein! Therefore, he is frustrated!

The Sage has accepted that at any moment they both have to be there. I had to accept whatever both 'do'. Why? Because neither 'does' anything. Both the good man and the bad man are body-mind organisms through which the Primal Energy functions, and brings about whatever is supposed to be brought about according to the Cosmic Law. So the Sage accepts whatever *Is*; the ordinary man keeps on choosing between one and the other and is, therefore, forever frustrated.

George: This situation here, like there, is... let's say there is a Sage who has accepted there is no doership and there are here all the egos who are in doership. Is that also a polarity?

Ramesh: Indeed! Indeed! Therefore, what this fresh conditioning produces will depend entirely on the Cosmic Law. Therefore, this fresh conditioning may amend and alter the existing conditioning in some, or not make any change at all in some, or result in total transformation. This is fresh conditioning which may go against a lot of existing conditioning. So, whether the existing conditioning is more powerful and throws out this fresh conditioning, or the fresh conditioning is powerful enough not only to change or amend but to totally transform, can happen only strictly according to a Cosmic Law.

Any questions?

George: I think that is good. I just wanted you to know that whether it is destiny or choice, I did not vote for George Bush.

(Ramesh and the room break out in laughter.)

Ramesh: You mean, you are a Democrat and not a Republican?

George: Yes, that is about right.

Ramesh: *(Laughing)* There, you made your choice! *(Laughing even more)*. There you made your choice! And my point, George, is on what basis did you make the choice? On the basis of your genes and your conditioning, make no mistake. You made the choice to be a Democrat and that choice was based on your genes and conditioning.

George: My parents, umm... I was raised in a Republican family.

Ramesh: Yes.

George: So?

Ramesh: You see, Republican and Democrat cannot be in the genes! Genes can only tell you, 'I simply cannot eat meat', the genes will prevent you. I will tell you a funny thing; you know when my younger son was born in 1948, in the same building two other children were born about the same time. My son is a Saraswat Brahmin, one of the other children is a Zoroastrian from a Parsi family, and one is from a Muslim family. Would you believe it? In spite of the Brahmin genes, my son always wanted... and, therefore, my wife took him on Saturday mornings to a good hotel and he had his chicken. Whereas the other two, George, believe it or not, a Parsi and a Muslim couldn't simply tolerate even meat being cooked in the house. See, even the genes have a limited way. They do have an effect, of course, but on the other hand, a friend of mine, who was a Gujarati with 100% vegetarian genes, told me when he went to England, 'No, now I am in England and I am trying to aspire to a good job in the Government when I go back, (*British government then*) therefore, I must be like an English man and I must eat meat.' So, one night he went to a small restaurant in London and ordered a meat dish. And he told me himself, he ate the first bite and he vomited all over the place! (*Laughing*) So, Republican or Democrat?! So, my point is even the genes have a limited effect.

George: *Thank you.*

Ramesh: So, genes plus conditioning. My point is, anything anyone thinks at any moment, George, my total acceptance is, anything anyone thinks at any moment depends on his programming – genes plus conditioning. Therefore, what I am saying is, I dare to say according to my concept, God created the programming – the genes and the conditioning – upon which depends what I think at any moment. Therefore, I think at any moment precisely what God wants me to think; let alone do!

George: *I think that is my resistance to the genetics and, somehow, I have it in a textbook and I don't see the divine connection with the genetics. And I think that is why I am having a resistance, when I hear you say it that way it resonates, it feels right.*

Ramesh: So, genes plus up to date conditioning. I say up to date because, as I told you, you heard me talk. This is fresh conditioning and the fresh conditioning may confirm what you already have or change or amend. So, the thoughts I have, action at any moment based on any thinking of mine, whatever I think at any moment, according to my concept, is based on programming and God made the programming! Therefore, at any moment, whatever I think, good or evil, is precisely what God wants me to think.

Do you remember a young man, eighteen years old, who went and shot the Israeli president Rabin some years ago? When he was in prison, one of the guards asked the young man, 'Why did you kill Rabin, a nice man, why did you kill him?' and he supposedly said, 'God made me do it.' And he was right. When he decided to kill, the thought, where could it have come from, except from God? So my point is, whatever one does, one does because that is his destiny and God's Will and the consequences, whatever they happen to be, are also God's Will. I do something because God wants me to do it, and the consequences, good, bad or indifferent, are also my destiny and God's Will.

George: So, there is no morality?

Ramesh: Morality is something created by the human being and the standards of morality, George, have differed all the time. Time and place determine morality. In one place only one wife, other places you can have two, three or more. What is morality? What is morality? Abortion, a few years ago, was a crime punishable by death in most countries. Today, the developing countries are sponsoring abortion. Government clinics, free abortion! Is abortion a good thing or is it a bad thing? Is it a moral or an immoral thing? So morality is a human concept, it changes from place and time. Then, if your conditioning and genes are to follow whatever is legal, you will follow the legal without thinking anything about it, but if your conditioning is that you will think you will go into this matter and then decide for yourself whether you will be an activist, or follow the agreed procedure. An activist is someone who has thought about it, disagreed with the existing view, and become an activist.

George: And it is all ok?

Ramesh: All ok, no! Ok or not is itself a question of morality but it is exactly as it is supposed to be according to the Cosmic Law. That is what I am saying. Right or wrong, I don't know. Moral or immoral, I don't know. All I am saying is, whatever *Is* at any moment is precisely what is supposed to be according to God's Will, according to a Cosmic Law. That is my point, and continuously judging what is right, what is wrong makes me frustrated! So, the privilege of judging, what is the privilege? Frustration!

George: Yes, sir.

Anil: I am Anil. Pediatrician by profession.

Ramesh: I see. I see.

Anil: What is love? I agree with your theory...

Ramesh: So, whatever you have heard now you have no objections, but you want to know why in all these (looking at the clock next to him) ninety minutes, I never used the word 'love'.

Anil: umm... I want to know what is love. That is all.

Ramesh: I see. Love, in life as we know it, is the absence of hate.

Anil: Right.

Ramesh: Love is absence of hate. 'I love somebody, I hate somebody.' 'I like someone, I dislike someone.' But if you are talking of the feeling, which arises when I meet someone; if I happen to be brought in the presence of a Sage, just in the presence of the Sage, a sense of love may arise in me. Therefore, the love arises; 'I' don't love or not love somebody. Love is a feeling which arises and if you want me to say what is love... your name you said is?

Anil: Anil.

Ramesh: So when love arises in the case of Anil, my concept is, whenever Anil feels like doing something for someone without expecting anything in return, you can call it love!

Anil: And this situation that you are talking about, we agree. Free will does not agree at the present moment. The situation that you are talking about, it happens momentarily or it happens with practice? If one goes on, accumulating more and more over time, you have to wait and watch, or is it a process and it suddenly happens?

Ramesh: What is the Ultimate Understanding? The Ultimate Understanding is 'no one is a doer'! That is the Ultimate Understanding. In most cases, normally, the understanding happens at an intellectual level. So I say, I cannot see how anyone cannot accept this concept because this concept means at one point, suddenly all my weight, all my burden of shame and guilt for my actions, and hatred and malice for the others' actions, that burden is immediately lifted. If I am not the doer, I see no point in feeling guilty about anything and if no one else is a doer, how can I hate him for anything? So, intellectually anybody can say, 'I cannot see how anybody cannot accept this concept which immediately removes my burden of shame and guilt and hatred and malice.' But, he confesses, it is only intellectually because deep down he is still not sure whether he is a doer or not, he is not sure. Then he may say, 'I am not sure because if you give me what they call a truth test serum which makes me speak the truth, and you ask me, 'Do I honestly believe no one is a doer', the answer may come 'Of course I do!' or 'I am not so sure'. Then that will tell me the level of acceptance.

Let's assume that it is only at the intellectual level, then I've got that conviction at the intellectual level and I would like it to be total. Now, even there I have to be sure. Do I really want it to be total or do I have a reservation? But, if I do want it to be total then is there a process?' My concept is, the basis of understanding is, the Total Understanding in any case, if it happens, is the destiny of that person or the Will of God. That is the bottom line. But having accepted that, while the sense of personal doership is still there, the ego-seeker asks me, 'Is there not something I can do? Accepting that the final understanding can only happen if it is God's Will and my destiny, in the meantime, is there not something I can do?' At this level, I tell him, 'Yes'.

According to my concept there is something you can do and that is at the end of the day, assuming you are busy throughout the day, take twenty or thirty minutes off, sit quietly and think of only one action which has happened during the day. Other actions, you may say, 'I am not too sure' but this one action, 'I am 100% sure this is my action!' Then, investigate that action. Investigate that 'Did I at any moment decide to do that action? How did that action begin?' And every single time, without exception, whether you investigate fifty actions or five hundred actions, every single time, without exception, the conclusion you will come to – if the investigation is total and honest – every single time will be, 'I did not at any particular time decide to do that'. 'In this particular action, a thought happened to me and because of that thought I did this', or 'I happened to see something at some moment and my happening to see something led to my action'.

In other words, every single time, without exception, the

conclusion you will come to is, 'If something had not happened over which I had no control, my action would not have happened.' Every single time. Do you see what I mean? If something earlier had not happened over which I had no control, what I now call my action would not have happened. Therefore, I cannot call it my action. Now how long this process from the intellectual level to the total level takes, is again God's Will and your destiny. But if you keep this process on, doing the investigation, honestly and thoroughly, my concept is at some point of time, depending on God's Will and your destiny, a sudden flash of acceptance will happen. A sudden flash, 'Of course I am not the doer!' Not 'I am not the doer', but the sudden flash is 'I cannot be the doer! And if I cannot be the doer, no one else can be the doer either!' But *when* this flow of acceptance happens, no one can know.

Therefore, from the intellectual level to the total level it is a process, it takes time and during that process, while the understanding is going deeper, the understanding will still function. Therefore, if at any moment you get involved as a doer, then in a conceptual scale of zero to ten, depending on the state at which your understanding is, you get involved at zero then you may remain involved, one, two, three right up to eight and then the understanding will cut it off. As the understanding goes deeper, the cutting off by the understanding, not you – you are the one who is involved – the stage at which the understanding cuts off gradually will become less and less. Eight, seven, six, five and as the understanding is nearing the total, you will find the involvement happening and the cutting off happening almost simultaneously. So, when you find that involvement happening, and the cutting off happening, then you can be sure you are very close to the Total Understanding. But this is a concept!

Day 3

Ramesh: Yes, Sudip?

Sudip: *Good morning. Today is my last day here.*

Ramesh: I see.

Sudip: *And I have three questions, perhaps if I can tell you all three, maybe they can all combine. One is a follow up of a question from the day before yesterday.*

Ramesh: I see. Yes.

Sudip: *I think in one stroke you threw away the law of causality.*

Ramesh: I am sorry?

Sudip: *You threw out the law of causality with the free will.*

Ramesh: No. Wait a minute, the two are entirely different. Law of causality says, 'An event happens, it will have its effect. The happening of one event will be the cause of the happening of another event. So, that which happens as an effect will be the cause of further events. But the events are the cause of one another, not anyone's deed.'

Sudip: And the effects are accrued to the doer then, according to the karma theory, are you throwing that out?

Ramesh: No. Individual karma theory I am throwing out. Causation I can't throw out.

Sudip: The effect then accrues to whom?

Ramesh: The effect accrues to whoever's destiny it is to be concerned with the event.

Sudip: Who is that entity?

Ramesh: That is the entity, which is identified with a particular name and form as a separate entity. The ego, the ego.

Sudip: When did the ego begin?

Ramesh: The ego begins according to my concept, around the age of two and two-and-a-half years in a baby. When the baby is born, and after a certain age, the child keeps on talking about himself or herself in the third person, 'he likes this, he does not like this, she likes this, she does not like this'. 'He' and 'she', but when the conditioning is strong enough and the child begins to use the personal pronoun 'me', then the ego has happened.

Sudip: What is the objective of pain, what is the purpose of creating the ego and the larger scheme of pain, which created obstacles to understand it?

Ramesh: Yes. That is the basis of life as we know it, inter-human relationships, and for inter-human relationships to happen, the ego has to be there. So, for life to happen, for the functioning of manifestation to happen, which is life as we know it, inter-human relationships have to happen. And for inter-human relationships to happen, egos – identified with a particular body-mind organism as a separate entity with a sense of doership – have to be there. And that identification with a particular name and form as a separate entity, according to my concept, must continue until the death of the body.

Suppose the understanding happens and a particular individual entity having totally accepted 'no one is a doer', let us say, becomes a Sage. The Sage in order to live the rest of his life has to respond to a name being called, he has to live his life, he has to practice his profession or occupation as a separate entity. So, my most important concept is, when an individual entity becomes a Sage, all that the Sage understands as a Sage is no one does anything. No 'one' does anything but the 'one' continues, has to continue to live the rest of his life, maybe in a different way, but the Sage has to live his life for the rest of his life. Therefore, the Sage must continue to live the rest of his life as a separate entity, make no mistake. So, my concept does not accept another concept which says, 'The moment a Sage becomes a Sage, no separation!' that doesn't happen. According to my concept, the separation has to be there; if a Sage deals with another person he has to accept 'he' is dealing with someone else. So, the separation between himself as a separate entity and some other person as a separate entity must continue.

Therefore, a Sage responds to his name being called, a Sage suffers the same pains and enjoys the same pleasures like anybody else, therefore, where is the difference between a Sage, who responds to his name being called, suffers the same pains and enjoys the same pleasures as an ordinary person, where is the difference? What makes a Sage, a Sage? The Sage has to continue to live his life as a separate entity, and to that extent separation has to be there, but what is understood totally is, 'no one is a doer', so what is destroyed in an ego, it is not separation as such. What is destroyed is a sense of personal doership but the destruction, annihilation of the sense of personal doership means, in effect, that the Sage has totally accepted 'no one is a doer'. Therefore, the doing happens as a result of the Primal Energy functioning through each of the billions of human body-mind organisms. The Primal Energy functions through each of these billion body-mind organisms and produces that event which is supposed to happen according to a Cosmic Law. Therefore, no one 'does' anything, whatever anybody thinks he does.

The Sage now understands it is not something done by him, but a happening brought about by the functioning of the Primal Energy through that body-mind organism. With that acceptance that no one does anything, one then continues to be a separate entity, has to, but the Sage sees each of the separate entities as separate instruments, separate robots through each of which the Primal Energy functions and brings about anything that is supposed to be brought about according to the Cosmic Law.

Then society decides some event is a good deed, another is a bad deed and the society rewards or punishes those deeds. So, the reward or the punishment for a particular body-mind organism as a separate entity is what I call that entity's destiny according to a Cosmic Law. So, a deed happens through a body-mind organism according to the Cosmic Law, and the reward or punishment for that action is also to be suffered by that entity according to the Cosmic Law. A deed happens which the ordinary person considers 'his' deed and, therefore, he says, 'my' deed has been appreciated by society or not appreciated by society. The Sage accepts a deed which has happened as God's Will and the result of it is also God's Will. So he doesn't say, 'I' did this and 'my' good deed was not appreciated', he merely sees a deed happens and the deed has a result. Both the happening of a deed and the result of that deed, the Sage accepts as part of the functioning of the Cosmic Law. No one is responsible and with this understanding the big deal, as far as the Sage is concerned, is when an action happens, he does not see it as 'somebody's action', therefore, he sees no reason to blame anybody.

In day-to-day living, from moment to moment, the Sage witnesses the happening of deeds or events but does not blame anyone; neither himself nor anyone else. So, the Sage continues to witness whatever happens in life as events and not somebody's deeds. With the result that the Sage is always free of blaming himself, which brings about a sense of shame or guilt, and he doesn't blame anybody else, therefore, there is no question of hatred and malice towards anybody. So, the Sage continues to live his life without blaming anybody and that is, according to my concept, the only difference between a Sage and an ordinary person.

Sudip: So, free will is a phantom, to think that we have free will is a total phantom apparently?

Ramesh: That is according to my concept and, more and more according to many scientists and psychologists also.

Sudip: Then would it not potentially bring in a sense of fatalism, which is so apparent in our culture anyway? We say, you know... 'make your life, go and work hard and do this'... so, there is a potential for fatalism, 'if I cannot control anything, if it happens it happens, I have to accept my lot in life'.

Ramesh: And, therefore, 'why should I get up from my bed and do anything?' That is fatalism, isn't it? What is fatalism?

Sudip: Or totally accepting, without any listening, what comes into one's life.

Ramesh: All right. That means either you can say, 'why should I get up from my bed?' which is fatalism, or you bring in the concept of responsibility. Why should anyone do anything with a sense of responsibility? 'I used to be a responsible person but now if I have to accept that no one does anything, then why should I live my life in a responsible manner? Why should I not live my life irresponsibly, like my friend does? He doesn't care a damn, when he has to make a decision he can't be bothered, he tosses a coin and he does it, so, I call him irresponsible. I don't do that! I am a responsible person. Therefore, what do I do? I consider the alternatives available to me very carefully, I consider the consequences of the various alternatives and then I decide in a responsible manner what to do. Therefore, I am a responsible person'. That is your idea of responsibility, isn't it?

My point is, a responsible person lives his life responsibly and makes his decisions responsibly, someone else tosses a coin, decides what to do and does it. As far as the results are concerned, does the responsible man have any control over the results of his actions? So, the question really is, why is a particular person responsible and why is someone else irresponsible, happy-go-lucky or whatever you call it? The answer is, the responsible man cannot help being responsible, the responsible man cannot be irresponsible if he wants to and the irresponsible person, even if he is told by everybody to be more responsible, he can't be responsible. Therefore, whether a man is responsible or irresponsible is part of his psychosomatic makeup. So, if the psychosomatic makeup makes someone responsible, because he accepts the principle 'no one is a doer' he cannot be irresponsible even if he wants to! And the irresponsible person is made to accept that he has to be responsible, then he decides to be, he makes a New Year's resolution, 'From now on I will be a very responsible person.' The first time he has to do anything, he tosses a coin! You see?

Responsibility. I have two aspects of responsibility. One is responsibility as far as society is concerned and that responsibility I can never give up. That is life. So, as far as responsibility to society is concerned, the Sage continues to accept responsibility for his actions. As far as society is concerned, the Sage accepts responsibility for his actions in this way – he accepts an action happens, 'my' action as far as society is concerned, has happened with God's Will according to a Cosmic Law, but nonetheless the Sage accepts that his action is his action and, therefore, he accepts the decision of society; the judgment of society, whether it is a good action or bad action. So, the Sage does not give up his responsibility for his actions as far as society is concerned, he can't! He has to live his life in society, he accepts that his actions will be rewarded or punished by society. But he accepts both the action and the results as God's Will according to the Cosmic Law.

Now, the other aspect is, his responsibility towards himself. It is his responsibility towards himself which makes him proud of his actions or feel a sense of guilt for his actions, one or the other. That responsibility to himself is totally demolished. An action happens, he accepts society's verdict because he has to live in society but as far as he is concerned, even if society decides that one of his actions is a bad action and punishes him, the Sage knowing that it is not 'his' action, will not carry a load of shame or guilt. So, the advantage of giving up his own responsibility, as far as he is concerned is, he doesn't carry a lot of shame and guilt for his action, nor hatred and malice towards anybody else, because it is not his action. Why is it not his action? Because the Sage accepts, 'If I am going to be hurt, I shall be hurt, because it is according to the Cosmic Law. If I am not going to be hurt, no power on earth can hurt me. If I am not going to be hurt because being hurt in a particular time and place is not my destiny, then no one can hurt me.'

Sudip: But it does not stop him from trying to take action according to so-called free will.

Ramesh: No. The action that happens...

Sudip: Apparent free will, to stop him from being hurt or something. He knows something is going to hurt him; he might take some steps to stop it. Prevent it.

Ramesh: He knows that if he puts his hand in the fire he will burn, so decides not to put his hand in the fire. He decides not to put the hand in the fire.

Sudip: Isn't that free will?

Ramesh: Oh! I see! So you have the free will to put your hand in the fire?

Sudip: Yes.

Ramesh: And would you do it?

Sudip: No, but isn't it free will that I choose not to?

Ramesh: No, if it were your free will, you would say 'I can do whatever...(?)' then put your hand in the fire, you won't! Sometimes, one time in ten times, you put your hand in the fire just to prove your free will! Just to prove your free will, Sudip, would you put your hand in the fire?

Sudip: No. Or clap, I mean I can decide to clap or not clap.

Ramesh: I see.

Sudip: And disturb this gathering.

Ramesh: Excellent. Now, you clap, 'you' clap, you know you will be disturbing others, knowing that would you clap? Knowing that you will be disturbing others, would you clap?

Sudip: I won't clap.

Ramesh: You won't. But clapping can happen! It has happened! I say something; the impact is so great you clap or you start getting up, laughing, smiling, whatever. Then, that is something that 'you' haven't done, it has happened. I'll tell you a story, quite a well known story. A king, who was a musician himself, quite often would have gatherings. He would have other singers sing and sometimes he would sing himself. And when he would sing, he noticed many of the people, you know would say 'wah, wah, wah', what a wonderful thing! You see he didn't want that. So what he said was, 'I am going to sing now and whoever says anything to disturb my singing is going to be executed.' Nobody says anything but a genuine music lover, when this king sings so well, the poor fellow can't help his 'wah, wah, wah'. So the king angrily said, 'Get up, come here!' and he comes shivering and what the king does is, he takes one of his necklaces out and puts it around his neck. Genuine music lover! Genuine music lover! He couldn't help it even if it meant his life. Even if it meant his life! I'll tell you another thing, that happened in a group which was with Ramana Maharshi.

Ramana Maharshi gave his concept 'everything is predetermined' and one of the persons then raised his arm and asked him, 'Is my raising my arm also predetermined?' and Ramana Maharshi said, 'Yes'. Unfortunately, there the conversation stopped, but if it had continued, I don't know whether Ramana Maharshi would have continued to give him a reason. I don't know but the reason for me is obvious. If Ramana Maharshi had not mentioned at that moment that everything is predetermined, would he have raised his arm? He wouldn't have raised his arm. So why did he raise his arm? What made him raise his arm? What made him raise his arm is some action over which he had no control, which was Ramana Maharshi saying everything is predetermined. So hearing everything is predetermined, the reaction of the hearing that something is predetermined is this action. So if that original saying, an action over which he had no control had not happened, which is Ramana Maharshi saying everything is predetermined, he would not have raised his arm. So it was predetermined that Ramana Maharshi would say at that moment 'everything is predetermined' and, therefore, it was also predetermined that he would raise his arm.

Sudip: Ramesh, just like you said two days ago that there is really no answer to 'why' the manifestation, on the same level, wouldn't it be right when we say we don't know why the ignorance of this individual, when really our source is knowledge anyway and we still feel ignorant? So, the ignorance had to begin sometime in a predetermined past, undetermined past. So, that too why, how can ignorance apparently come out of all knowledge. Does it have an answer?

Ramesh: Yes. The answer is that at any moment everything is What Is according to a Cosmic Law. Why is What Is, means you want to know the basis on which the Cosmic Law functions. The basis on which the Cosmic Law functions and has been functioning for since time immorial, no one can know. No one can know. The Cosmic Law refers to all eternity, so the cause and effect over eternity which the Cosmic Law knows, how can anyone know? That is why, you know, when Niels Bohr and his colleagues presented to Albert Einstein the new theory, the Theory of Uncertainty, that no one truly knows what is going to happen in the future, Niels Bohr asked Albert Einstein if he had any scientific objections.

Albert Einstein confessed he went through it very thoroughly and, he used the German expression, 'I couldn't put a needle through it', the theory is 100% per cent correct, but he said, 'I simply cannot accept that implication of your theory which is that God plays dice with the universe. Nothing is certain. I cannot accept that God plays dice with the universe'. Then Niels Bohr gave him an answer, he said, 'God does not play dice with the universe. We think God plays dice with the universe because we do not have the full information which God has about eternity!' We do not, and we cannot, have the information which God has.

Sudip: Acceptance of the facts seems difficult sometimes but we 'cannot never' want to know what the purpose of life is, and we cannot go through life as a robot. That acceptance seems to be the difficulty. Somehow, in the intellectual mind, you want to try to find answers to everything, not to give up that quest.

Ramesh: Yes. So it is difficult, difficult for most people, is that what you are saying?

Sudip: Yes, to let go of the quest.

Ramesh: So why is that? Why would it be so difficult for most people to accept this intellectually but not totally? Why is it easy to accept intellectually, because intellectually I get, 'If I do not blame anyone for any deed, then I never have to feel guilty or ashamed of anything nor hate anyone else. Therefore, if I am able to accept totally, 'no one does anything', then at one point, at one stroke, all my burden of shame and guilt for my actions and hatred and malice for the others may be removed'. Isn't that fantastic? Therefore, intellectually it is not difficult but to give up a concept of free will, which has been established for thousands of years, it is not easy. Why is the position this, that I accept it intellectually but not totally? Because, if everyone was able to accept it totally, life as we know it wouldn't happen. For life to happen, interhuman relationships have to happen and interhuman relationships happen because each one blames someone for something that has happened. If no one blamed anybody, neither himself nor anybody else for anything, how could life as we know it ever happen? Some day, could it happen? God knows! At the moment it doesn't.

Therefore, why is a Sage, a Sage? Because that is what's God's Will. According to a Cosmic Law, at any moment there have to be so many Sages; not one will be less nor one will be more. Therefore, I say, the happening of a Sage, the happening of the event of self-realization or enlightenment is an impersonal happening, happening through a particular body-mind organism. Therefore, no one can aim to or achieve self-realization. If it is to happen, it will happen. The very fact of wanting to achieve it is the biggest problem. The biggest obstacle to the happening of self-realization is that the individual wants to achieve it and it can't be achieved, it can only happen. It can only happen, if it is supposed to happen, according to a Cosmic Law.

Sudip: The best thing that the person can do is to wait patiently or create certain circumstances, where this can happen?

Ramesh: And then still wait patiently! Wait patiently. More importantly, wait patiently without expectation, that is the point. The relevant point is, wait patiently without expectation. It is the expectation which produces frustration.

Sudip: Swami ji, we say... I said 'swami ji' I am sorry.

Ramesh: Ok, I don't take it as an insult.

Sudip: No, but it is a title. It is out of respect.

Ramesh: Yes.

Sudip: We are conditioned through saying, 'God is all loving, God is always benevolent.'

Ramesh: 'God is all knowing, all powerful, all merciful!'

Sudip: Loving is a better aspect that I could take but isn't it more true to the Absolute that what is, is, and just apply or project our value system to it?

Ramesh: Yes, therefore, what you are saying is absolutely correct. God is a concept created by the human being and the human being wants someone to beg to for something. So the human being has created the concept of God, and then given him attributes, 'all knowing, all powerful, all merciful'. So, 'I' create a concept of God, 'I' provide him with the attribute of all merciful and then 'I' ask him, 'God, why are you creating handicapped children?' That is what is happening. Whereas, God could tell someone... the only thing God would tell you is, 'The basis of manifestation and His functioning is the existence at any moment, and every moment, of duality.' The existence of both the interconnected opposites of every conceivable kind, which make up What Is in any moment, is precisely what is supposed to be. Therefore, God would say, 'If you keep on choosing one against the other, you will continue to be frustrated and unhappy.' Then if you want to say something God would have disappeared because God has told you all he can tell you! You choose one against the other, you will be unhappy and frustrated and God would disappear. He has told you all he can tell you, more than that he can tell you nothing.

Sudip: To accept the whole thing in totality, the whole duality, the opposites, the whole thing?

Ramesh: In other words, what I am saying is, if you put it in words – I have heard many people say, 'no, you can't put it in words', why not? What I am saying is, all you have to do is to be able to accept What Is at any moment as something which is there. To 'be able' to accept, whether you are able to accept or not, is God's Will according to Cosmic Law and your destiny!

Sudip: But is there any role for prayer? For idol worship? For going to the temple ten times a day, whatever, or fasting? What people do in an effort to reach that understanding. Is there any role for all this?

Ramesh: Yes. They do whatever they are doing; prayers in the morning, self-discipline during the day, celibacy during the night and being celibate all these years, and at one point they say, 'What have I achieved? All I have achieved is, starve myself of sex for thirty years!' I'll tell you a joke. You know, there was a Buddhist monastery, a new monk was given a sutra to copy, copy it fifty times. The monk noticed that what he had was a copy, so the student went to the head monk and said, 'Look, this is a copy, if there is a mistake in that copy, I will be continuing the mistake for fifty other copies. Wouldn't it be better if we go to the archives and compare it with the original, and see whether there is a mistake and then have fifty correct copies?' The head monk said, 'That is a good idea. It hasn't struck me before.' So, the head monk goes to the archives, doesn't come up for quite sometime, half an hour, one hour. So, the monk goes down to see, 'I hope he has not fainted or something.' So, he goes down and finds his head monk weeping bitterly, weeping bitterly! So, he says, 'What is the matter?' So, the head monk between his sobs tells him, 'The word is *celebrate!*'

Sudip: So, Ramesh, there is not much role in this to get to the understanding.

Ramesh: Sorry?

Sudip: There is not much role for all these different things people do. What are they trying to do?

Ramesh: No. What I am saying Sudip is, 'they' are not doing it, it is happening because it is supposed to happen in their lives as their destiny. If it is the destiny of someone to do all this and be frustrated at the end of thirty years, that will happen. That is part of What Is. So many people doing what we have just said, that is part of What Is. So, that one is a spiritual seeker is itself his destiny. Who is going to be a spiritual seeker and who is going to be a seeker after money or fame or power has already been decided, and your body-mind organism has been duly programmed for that seeking to happen. So, if it is your destiny to be a spiritual seeker, your body-mind organism has been appropriately programmed for that seeking to happen. Then the seeking begins. What course the seeking will take is your destiny. So, whether it is your destiny to go straight to someone whose concept appeals to you, accept it and not face more frustration or whether you go through a winding road, through one guru after another guru, one frustration after another frustration, that will be your destiny. So, if one is supposed to go through that for many years, and then go to a sane guru, then that is what will happen. But if someone goes straight there, that is it.

There was a twenty-year-old French student, twenty years old, can you believe it? He asked questions and finally, at one point, that is it! Twenty-year-old student! Along with him was a twenty-two-year-old British student. Two of them sitting side by side asking, very deliberately, questions and because they were not loaded with a lot of knowledge they were very open, very receptive and both of them accepted, you see? The French student had come with his father, neither of them knew English, so father and son came here with an interpreter. After a while, the interpreter was interested too. Then the father said about his son, 'He is the one who is interested.' So, gradually, he got the understanding. I think he got the understanding and for the rest of his life it is there. Then he went back to France for his studies, and do you know he came back after two weeks and once I was telling people, 'Gilles went and came back after two or three weeks'. 'Not three, two' he corrected me. Came back after two weeks! He said, 'I just felt I had to come!' And the second time he was here, not a peep out of him. He just sat there smiling and there was a tremendous difference on his face. First time he came, furrows and worry; second time he came, lovely face.

Sudip: Is there a role for meditation then in this? That is a little different.

Ramesh: No. There is no difference. There is a role for meditation if your destiny includes that role. The big difference is, 'intellectually I can't not accept it, deep down I am not so sure.' Then for the intellectual acceptance to go deep, the only spiritual practice I recommend is, at the end of the day, assuming you have been busy during the day, take twenty, thirty minutes off, sit quietly and select only one action during the day, which you are convinced is your action, but just one action. Then investigate it thoroughly and honestly, 'Did I at any particular moment decide to do that action? How did that action happen?' Then you will come to the conclusion, 'I had a thought', and you have no control over the thought which happened, 'I had a thought which led to my action'. Therefore, your investigation tells you, if that thought had not occurred over which you had no control, your action would not have happened. I tell you with confidence, you can investigate as many actions as you want and every time, without a single exception, you will find that the cause of your action was some event over which you had no control.

You happened to see something, you happened to hear something, you happened to read something, you happened to smell something, taste something, catch something which resulted in your action. And every single time you will come to the conclusion if that had not happened, your action would not have happened. How can you call it your action? And depending on your destiny, at some point during this investigation, it is more than likely that a flash of total acceptance will happen, 'I cannot be the doer' not 'I am not the doer'. 'I cannot be the doer and if I cannot be the doer, no one else can be a doer either.' When it happens, it is your destiny. That is the only spiritual practice I recommend. Then someone says, 'I have been practicing meditation for a long time, should I stop it?' So, I say, 'No. Why are you meditating regularly?' 'I like it.' 'Wonderful, so enjoy it as something you like and not something which you are compelled to do.' So, if you have been meditating for thirty years feeling compelled to do it and wishing that you would not be doing it, then you can stop it. Or more than likely I tell him, 'Having heard this new concept, meditation might just drop off, then don't feel guilty.'

Sudip: So Ramesh, is there any connection between enlightenment and miracles? In India, as you know, there are so many people who claim they are, or they think they are, enlightened with certain things they do which gathers a lot of crowd. So, does enlightenment bring about certain powers in the physical abilities as well? Or, what is the whole relationship?

Ramesh: There is no relationship. From my concept, which is incidentally exactly the same as the Buddha's, what is my basic concept? What the Buddha said was, 'Events happen, deeds are done, there is no individual doer thereof' and then he said, 'Enlightenment, what is enlightenment?' Buddha is very clear, five words, 'Enlightenment means end of suffering!' Very sure. So, what does he mean by suffering? What is the suffering which enlightenment brings the end of? What is the suffering which no longer remains once enlightenment has happened? Does it mean I no longer have pain in my life? It can't be so. Therefore, my concept here is, Buddha could not possibly have meant, the end of suffering which you, as an animal, must suffer along with other animals, but that the suffering which will end is that which the animal does not know. The suffering, which the animal knows and 'I' as an animal must suffer, will continue because that is part of life. The suffering that Buddha says ends is the suffering which the animal does not have. See what I mean? The only suffering Buddha could have meant is that suffering which the animal doesn't know. So what is the suffering, which the animal doesn't know but the human being knows and doesn't want? That suffering is the suffering created, according to my concept, by the sense of personal doership. The animal does everything, he has an ego, if he has food he will guard it. So, a separate entity the animal certainly has, but the animal does not have a sense of personal doership. Therefore, the animal does not suffer from a load of guilt and shame or a load of hatred and malice towards anyone. So, that suffering which the Buddha meant, is obviously the suffering which the animal does not suffer but is only the dubious advantage the human being enjoys, to suffer guilt and shame and hatred and malice.

Whether any gifts arise after enlightenment depends on the Cosmic Law. But one thing, if there is a Sage, a proper Sage who truly accepts no one is a doer, then the gifts that arise will be accepted not as 'my' gifts but the gifts that are supposed to go with this body-mind organism which will be used by God whenever necessary.

Once, a woman came to Ramana Maharshi with a child that was

almost dying. She laid the child beside her and just sat there praying, you can say, to Ramana Maharshi. Very soon the child got up and the child became absolutely normal again. Everybody around was most impressed and the woman of course was devastated, she kept on thanking Ramana Maharshi and ultimately picked up the child and left. Do you know what Ramana Maharshi's reaction was? He said, 'There was not even a 'sankalpa', I did not even have a wish that he would get well. It happened.' Why did it happen? It was the destiny of the woman and her son or grandson. So, if a gift arises, the gift will work itself whenever it is supposed to work according to the Cosmic Law. The Sage who has the full understanding, in whom the gift arises, will not consider it as 'his' gift. But what gift can arise no one can know. Or no gift can arise, then the really wise Sage will be very happy if no gift arises.

Sudip: So, really, the other should not judge if a person is enlightened or not depending upon whether he has extra powers.

Ramesh: That is it exactly. The only standard to judge whether a man is a Sage or not is to see his behavior, not behavior as such, but his reaction to whatever happens. (And his reaction to whatever happens he would have understood). A Sage you have seen, many people say, getting angry, and people say, 'He gets angry every now and then, how can he be a Sage? He smokes 'bidis', how can he be a Sage? He eats tobacco, how can he be a Sage? He is a non-vegetarian, how can he be a Sage?' Arising of anger, how does the Sage see it? The Sage witnesses anger arising, or whatever arises, anger arising, fear arising, compassion arising, in 'a' body-mind organism, whether it arises in A, B, C, or himself, is immaterial! It is a reaction which arises in a body-mind organism when one of the senses comes in contact with its relevant object. Eyes see something, ears hear something, there is a reaction and that belongs to the body-mind organism, and that reaction in that body-mind organism has a reason because that body-mind organism has been programmed to have that reaction. So the

Sage does not see anything happening as 'your' action or 'my' action but as an arising. So, if the Sage really understands no one is a doer, then the main point, as I understand is, he doesn't blame anybody for any action. That is the core of my concept of what constitutes enlightenment.

Sudip: I have no more questions.

ॐ

Ramesh: Would you pass it (*the mike*) on? Press and then clip. Yes. That is enough. Your name is?

Jollean: Jollean Sandwell.

Ramesh: I see. Yes, Jollean.

Jollean: And I am from Canada.

Ramesh: Now, you came from Canada, French part or the English part?

Jollean: English. And my teacher, Esther, wanted to send you greetings and warm hugs. She saw you about seven years ago and her husband John.

Ramesh: They are both healers.

Jollean: He has developed a body work system.

Ramesh: Yes. I know, they were here. And what do you do in life?

Jollean: That is what I do. I am a body work instructor. I met them two years ago and that is the first time I started to know anything about this philosophy. Up until that time, I was searching for God since I was very, very, very little and then...

Ramesh: Since you were very, very ill?

Jollean: Little. Tiny.

Ramesh: Yes. Yes, that is, as far back as you can remember you have been a seeker. So, have you ever wondered Jollean what you have been seeking?

Jollean: Always. Ummm... I think, well, many kinds of things, I am thinking... some connection with God and I would be thinking about that, I would think, 'that I would be a kind person and then I would be able to help people and then ummm... (crying) it would be worthwhile to stay here.'

Ramesh: Yes. So was your intention then to be able to help people?

Jollean: It was, yes.

Ramesh: You expected enlightenment to give you the gift of healing. Is that what you mean? You expected that enlightenment would give you the valued gift of helping people?

Jollean: But I didn't look at it as enlightenment because I didn't know about that word.

Ramesh: Yes. As far as you are concerned, what you wanted God to give you was the power to heal.

Jollean: Yes, because my mum... I used to 'do' my mum's headaches when I was really little, and she always used to tell me that I could grow and help people that way. (crying)

Ramesh: I see. Migraine headaches?

Jollean: My mum did. Yes. So, I just have this in my heart, there is always this burning, just to know, I just wanted to know...

Ramesh: To be able to cure people, help people. Now you are able to do that, to the extent that you are supposed to.

Jollean: (Laughing) Yes.

Ramesh: Now do you want anything or have you got what you were seeking for in life? Now, at this moment, being able to heal people, is there something that you are still seeking or is it over?

Jollean: Well, obviously, because I think probably the whole thing was to heal myself.

Ramesh: Yes.

Jollean: And the rest would...

Ramesh: Heal yourself. Heal yourself, Jollean, of what?

Jollean: I could never figure that out. But it just seemed to me since I was little, that if I understood, if I could just understand, then my life would be different.

Ramesh: Yes. Yes. In what way would your life be different, Jollean? That is what I am saying. So far you have not understood, now you have understood... having understood whatever you wanted to understand, in what way would your life, henceforth, be different and more acceptable?

Jollean: It is like I understand intellectually, you know, little... ok? Because I haven't gone to school past secondary education and I've always felt that my brain doesn't understand enough.

Ramesh: I see.

Jollean: My heart understands but... (crying)

Ramesh: Actually, Jollean, what you are seeking is not to be understood by your brain but to be accepted by your heart. So, to understand what I am talking about you don't need a lot of brain, in fact, actually I think, not too active a brain is a very good thing! Therefore, Jollean, many people who are able to accept it with their brain are still looking for something deeper! So, if you can stop the intervening intellectual, so much the better! So, deeply understanding with the heart, my concept, Jollean, is very simple. If your heart can accept that everything that happens is a happening created by God according to a Cosmic Law and no one does anything, that is the only understanding according to my concept which is necessary. All else is knowledge, information, not really necessary. That is my concept. All that one has to truly accept with the heart is, no one is a doer! No one can do anything because anything anyone thinks 'he' or 'she' has done is truly a happening, brought about by God according to a Cosmic Law.

Then the question is, 'How can it be a big deal?' By accepting no one is a doer, that is all enlightenment means, then what is the advantage of enlightenment? What has enlightenment done for me if I am truly able to accept? That is the question asked by the brain, Jollean, the heart doesn't ask it. If the heart has accepted it, the heart knows the advantage. The heart knows the big deal of what we are talking about. The heart knows that because the heart has been able to accept no one is a doer, the heart does not have to carry the big burden of shame and guilt for his or her own actions nor hatred and malice for anyone else's actions. So the heart, having accepted it, does not have this question. 'What advantage do I get?', but the intellect still wants to know what is the big deal. So it is the intellect that has to be told that if the heart is able to accept it, you will no longer carry the burden of pride and arrogance for 'my' good deeds, guilt and shame for 'my' bad deeds, hatred and malice towards the other for 'his' or 'her' deeds. So if the heart has accepted it, then the heart knows what it has already achieved, there is no more load of shame and guilt or hatred and malice and the heart is satisfied.

Jollean: You make it seem simple when I hear you talk. Simple. When I listened to others it was so difficult to understand, because of the mind stuff, and I just always was at a loss.

Ramesh: So the important thing as I see it, Jollean, is, not to have any concepts and the heart accepts only one thing – I don't do anything, no one else does anything either. Therefore, there is no need for me to blame myself for any action or anyone else for any action, that is all. Truly, it is as simple as that.

Jollean: I thought I had to go to school to learn.

Ramesh: I am sorry?

Jollean: I thought I would have to go to school and get a PhD. or something.

Ramesh: Yes, to satisfy your intellect (*Laughing*), the heart doesn't need any education. Yes.

Jollean: So, I heard that sometimes you tell people how long they should come to you. Somebody told me that in Canada. I am here for two weeks and...

Ramesh: If somebody asks me, somebody has asked, 'How long do I think someone has to be here' and I say, 'Three days. Three days!'

Jollean: Three days.

Ramesh: First day, to understand what I talked about. Second day, to weigh the concept that I have because if I tell you in one day and you accept it, then I don't want it to be a brain washing.

So on the first day you hear what I am saying, then that afternoon you think about it, question it, truly question it and then questioning it you may have certain questions. Bring up those questions the next day and when those are answered, the third day one or two questions may remain and when we deal with that, ten minutes on the third day, everything is clear. And that is truly what happened once with a Buddhist monk, a regular monk. He came here, he sat for a day for the first time, listened to everything, no questions except to get some point clarified, just listened, no expression on his face. Second day, he came with a long list of questions, long list and we went through it, question by question, and he questioned me on every one of those questions. Therefore, he was not being brain washed. Third day, he came with just two questions, finished in ten minutes.

The people who were watching this noticed a tremendous difference in the face of the Buddhist monk. First day, he sat there practicing serenity, practicing serenity, you see, and in that serenity he created a lot of... (*pointing to creases on the forehead*), when the questions arose... (*pointing to different creases*) and when he left there was such an expression of purity on his face that at the end of the third talk, friends of mine, Italian friends of mine, each said to the other, remarked a similar thing, at the end of the third talk, there was such an expression on his face which each of them interpreted 'As if he had seen the Buddha.' That was the expression you see? And if you want to know more about it, there is a book called 'Advaita, The Buddha and the Unbroken Whole'. That book really concerns just three talks. So, you are going to be here for what?

Jollean: Two weeks.

Ramesh: So, after the fourth day what are you going to do, Jollean?

Jollean: (Laughing)

Ramesh: I suggest you go to Goa.

Jollean: So, if I can come back here on the fourth day does that mean that I am just not getting it, or what? Not intelligent enough, or what? (Laughing)

Ramesh: Good question, Jollean. (*Laughing*) Good question.

Jollean: So can I ask you a question about God? If everything that we talk about is a concept... why?

Ramesh: Yes. Good question, again! What is the truth? The question, Jollean, really is, that if everything is a concept is there any truth in life or phenomenality? I go further in there, what I say, Jollean, is, anything any Sage has ever said, Christ or Moses or Mohammed or Ramana Maharshi, anything any Sage has ever said, is a concept. Anything any scripture of any religion has said is a concept. A concept being something that some people accept, some people will deny. The truth is something which no one can deny. So on the basis that 'that' cannot be denied by anybody, can there be a truth do you think? According to my concept, there IS one truth which nobody can deny and that is, the impersonal awareness of being, I Am, I exist. That is the only truth which cannot disappear. For instance, someone comes, some accident happens, he loses all his memory, all total memory is completely wiped out and yet this will not be wiped out. He will forget who he is, where he is, but he cannot forget that he Is, 'I Am', I exist. That, which no accident can erase, is the only truth, 'I Am', I exist, everything else is a concept.

Jollean: So, before I was so-called born, I existed?

Ramesh: 'I', not as Jollean. That is the point. Not as Jollean. What was born was a body-mind organism subsequently named Jollean.

Jollean: And so when I so called die, then?

Ramesh: Then Jollean will be exactly what she was before she was born! And for that reason, I see no reason why Jollean should ever worry about that.

Jollean: I don't actually. I have lived a long time.

Ramesh: So, dying means going back home. Dying means going back to where I was before birth took place. So what has been there always is this impersonal awareness of being. When we think in terms of that separate entity all the problems arise, and yet each of us has to live his or her life as a separate entity.

Jollean: So, this philosophy is so, in one way, so simple then why? Mmm... that is a 'why' question. How come that is...

Ramesh: Is it so difficult to accept?

Jollean: Yes, but here, it seems it goes down to about here (pointing to a point in her body) and...

Ramesh: Big block.

Jollean: Yes, because it seems so easy. If I really totally accepted that, I would have no more guilt, I would have no more blame, I would have no more shame, I wouldn't be angry at anybody because I would know that they are just doing what is in the body-mind to do and myself, then it would be like total freedom and...

Ramesh: Yes, but wait a minute, just one small clarification. You said, 'I won't get angry anymore', anger will arise but Jollean would not be involved in that anger as 'her' being angry. You see? So subject to that, anger may arise, compassion may arise. If anger arises, Jollean will not say, 'I was angry, I shouldn't be angry.' If compassion arises, Jollean will not say, 'I am a compassionate person.' So, whatever normal biological reaction appears in the body-mind organism, Jollean wouldn't get involved in it as a person. In other words, this total acceptance of no one does anything, means merely witnessing whatever reaction – natural, biological reaction – arises in 'any' body. Therefore, whatever reaction arises in this body, I don't blame myself. If anger or whatever arises in another body-mind organism, I don't blame the other person either. It is a natural biological reaction arising in a body-mind organism precisely the way it is supposed to.

Jollean: So, it seems like that is the way to live!

Ramesh: That is the point.

Jollean: And so the intellect says, 'That is the way to live' then I believe it in my heart and soul that is the way to live and, yet, am I living that way all the time? No. So, what is stopping me from...

Ramesh: Your destiny. God's Will. God's Will yes, but that shouldn't make you pessimistic, Jollean. Why? Because, that you have been a spiritual seeker since your childhood was not your doing.

Jollean: I know.

Ramesh: So, the fact that you were a spiritual seeker from your childhood was something made by God. So God started this body-mind organism as a seeker since she was a child, since then you have done whatever reading you have done and your being here is precisely because God wanted you to be here, otherwise you wouldn't be here. So, because of God's Will you have been a spiritual seeker, you are here and you have listened to my concept. So I see no reason why this concept should not ultimately be accepted in your heart. God started the seeking, let him deal with it.

Jollean: Ok.

Ramesh: Let him deal with it! Which means I see no reason why Jollean should keep on wondering, 'When is it going to happen?' Let it happen if it happens, otherwise it won't happen. Who cares? (*Laughing*) There is a book called 'Who Cares?!'; good book. You know how the title 'Who Cares?!' came? It contains a story, the story is: one spiritual seeker went to a master. He was there, he thought he had understood and he decided that he would go back and write a letter every month to his guru. So, the first letter came and he said, 'All this is merely an illusion, created by the Source...' and this, that and the other. The guru looked at it, threw it away. Another month, another letter, another aspect of noumenon and phenomenality and all that kind of garbage. Again the guru threw it away. Then suddenly the letters ceased. So, after about an interval of six months, the guru realized no letters were coming, so he wrote to him. He said, 'I thought you were going to send me a report every month, why have you not done it?' and the letter came back, 'Who cares?' Then the guru was delighted!

But you will be here for some time, so any time you want you are most welcome. The question is, why should Jollean come again and again after three or four days when she's got it. What is the answer, Jollean?

Jollean: Oh, it is just so nice to be here!

Ramesh: Ah! You know my answer is, I hear a piece of music, I have listened to Leonard Cohen's new disc, 'Ten New Songs', and actually fallen in love with it. I listened to it again and again, why? I have heard it, I know it is good. Why do I listen to it again and again? I like it! Therefore, why should I not listen to something which I like? Why should I not eat something which I like? I have eaten and thought it was great, why do I eat again? I like it!

Jollean: Ok.

Ramesh: (*Talking to the next person adjusting the mike*) I think that if you clip it on top, it will be better. Yes. Yes, sir. Your name is?

Paul: Paul. I don't have a question. I am just very happy to be here.

Ramesh: Good.

Paul: A lot of gratitude and...

Ramesh: How long have you been here? Yesterday and today?

Paul: Yes.

Ramesh: I see, and what is your reaction Paul? Are you inclined to accept whatever is said?

Paul: Yes.

Ramesh: No questions?

Paul: No.

Ramesh: Ok. How long are you going to be here?

Paul: Tomorrow I leave. My third day, no, no... I will be here I think a week or so.

Ramesh: I see. So any time questions arise, you are welcome to sit in the chair and ask a question and we go through it, ok?

Paul: Yes, I'd like to say one thing; the sense of presence when the involvement stops, you know, there is a sense of presence.

Ramesh: Yes, indeed.

Paul: And that sense of presence is like the attention becomes more acclimated to identify with that presence rather than the stream.

Ramesh: Than with Paul.

Paul: Yes, than with Paul.

Ramesh: In other words, what you are saying, Paul, is, in between the two involvements there is a gap which means a sense of independent, impersonal presence. So, that impersonal sense of presence means Paul at that moment, is not there. That is the impersonal awareness, the I Am, that I am talking about, which is the Source. So, therefore, the more you are able to be in that sense of presence, the less problems you will have but you can't be in that sense of presence all the time. Paul has to work and earn a living, so the question, therefore, is how can Paul live his life, earn his living, deal with what happens in society and yet be in that presence? You see? And my point is, you live your life without blaming yourself or blaming anybody. So, if you can live your life without blaming yourself or anybody for anything that is happening then you are slightly, further, gradually further, back from your presence. So, when you are able to accept whatever happens as something which had to happen and not blame anybody then, for practical purposes, Paul as identified consciousness will be further and further behind. My point, Paul, is, you don't have to keep remembering about your impersonal presence, you don't! It is there whether you like it or not. Similarly, you have a home, you leave in the morning, what do you do in life, Paul?

Paul: As little as possible.

Ramesh: How do you earn your living?

Paul: I am a building contractor.

Ramesh: I see. So in the morning you leave your home, go to a contract site, to a construction site and there you spend the day.

Working, giving instructions, doing something yourself. When you are doing that you don't keep reminding yourself where your home is, do you? You don't have to. Your home is where it is. So, the impersonal presence is always there. So, my point is you don't have to think that you must be in that presence all the time. Just as you don't have to remember where your home is when you are working, you work and do whatever you want and the impersonal sense of presence is always there. You don't have to remember it. That is my point. It is always there. Fine. So, if any questions arise, bring them up again.

OTHER RAMESH BALSEKAR TITLES
PUBLISHED BY YOGI IMPRESSIONS

For information on Ramesh Balsekar, visit:
www.rameshbalsekar.com

For further details, contact:
Yogi Impressions Books Pvt. Ltd.
1711, Centre 1, World Trade Centre,
Cuffe Parade, Mumbai 400 005, India.

Fill in the Mailing List form on our website
and receive, via email, information on
books, authors, events and more.
Visit: www.yogiimpressions.com

Telephone: (022) 61541500, 61541541
Fax: (022) 61541542
E-mail: yogi@yogiimpressions.com

 Join us on Facebook:
www.facebook.com/yogiimpressions

Made in the USA
Coppell, TX
08 May 2021

55286098R00066